D0628911

PENGUIN POPULAR CLASSICS

# AS YOU LIKE IT

## WILLIAM SHAKESPEARE

PENGUIN BOOKS

# PENGUIN BOOKS

Published by the Penguin Group
Penguin Books Ltd, 27 Wrights Lane, London W8 5TZ, England
Penguin Putnam Inc., 375 Hudson Street, New York, New York 10014, USA
Penguin Books Australia Ltd, Ringwood, Victoria, Australia
Penguin Books Canada Ltd, 10 Alcorn Avenue, Toronto, Ontario, Canada M4V 3B2
Penguin Books (NZ) Ltd, Private Bag 102902, NSMC, Auckland, New Zealand

Penguin Books Ltd, Registered Offices: Harmondsworth, Middlesex, England

Published in Penguin Popular Classics 1994
9

Copyright 1937, 1946 by the Estate of G. B. Harrison

Printed in England by Cox & Wyman Ltd, Reading, Berkshire

# CONTENTS

# THE WORKS OF SHAKESPEARE

## PLAYS

| APPROXIMATE DATE | | FIRST PRINTED |
|---|---|---|
| Before 1594 | HENRY VI *three parts* | Folio 1623 |
| | RICHARD III | 1597 |
| | TITUS ANDRONICUS | 1594 |
| | LOVE'S LABOUR'S LOST | 1598 |
| | THE TWO GENTLEMEN OF VERONA | Folio |
| | THE COMEDY OF ERRORS | Folio |
| | THE TAMING OF THE SHREW | Folio |
| 1594–1597 | ROMEO AND JULIET (*pirated* 1597) | 1599 |
| | A MIDSUMMER NIGHT'S DREAM | 1600 |
| | RICHARD II | 1597 |
| | KING JOHN | Folio |
| | THE MERCHANT OF VENICE | 1600 |
| 1597–1600 | HENRY IV *part i* | 1598 |
| | HENRY IV *part ii* | 1600 |
| | HENRY V (*pirated* 1600) | Folio |
| | MUCH ADO ABOUT NOTHING | 1600 |
| | MERRY WIVES OF WINDSOR (*pirated* 1602) | Folio |
| | AS YOU LIKE IT | Folio |
| | JULIUS CÆSAR | Folio |
| | TROYLUS AND CRESSIDA | 1609 |
| 1601–1608 | HAMLET (*pirated* 1603) | 1604 |
| | TWELFTH NIGHT | Folio |
| | MEASURE FOR MEASURE | Folio |
| | ALL'S WELL THAT ENDS WELL | Folio |
| | OTHELLO | 1622 |
| | LEAR | 1608 |
| | MACBETH | Folio |
| | TIMON OF ATHENS | Folio |
| | ANTONY AND CLEOPATRA | Folio |
| | CORIOLANUS | Folio |
| After 1608 | PERICLES (*omitted from the Folio*) | 1609 |
| | CYMBELINE | Folio |
| | THE WINTER'S TALE | Folio |
| | THE TEMPEST | Folio |
| | HENRY VIII | Folio |

## POEMS

| DATES UNKNOWN | | |
|---|---|---|
| | VENUS AND ADONIS | 1593 |
| | THE RAPE OF LUCRECE | 1594 |
| | SONNETS } | 1609 |
| | A LOVER'S COMPLAINT } | |
| | THE PHŒNIX AND THE TURTLE | 1601 |

# WILLIAM SHAKESPEARE

William Shakespeare was born at Stratford upon Avon in April, 1564. He was the third child, and eldest son, of John Shakespeare and Mary Arden. His father was one of the most prosperous men of Stratford who held in turn the chief offices in the town. His mother was of gentle birth, the daughter of Robert Arden of Wilmcote. In December, 1582, Shakespeare married Ann Hathaway, daughter of a farmer of Shottery, near Stratford; their first child Susanna was baptized on May 6, 1583, and twins, Hamnet and Judith, on February 22, 1585. Little is known of Shakespeare's early life; but it is unlikely that a writer who dramatized such an incomparable range and variety of human kinds and experiences should have spent his early manhood entirely in placid pursuits in a country town. There is one tradition, not universally accepted, that he fled from Stratford because he was in trouble for deer stealing, and had fallen foul of Sir Thomas Lucy, the local magnate; another that he was for some time a schoolmaster.

From 1592 onwards the records are much fuller. In March, 1592, the Lord Strange's players produced a new play at the Rose Theatre called *Harry the Sixth*, which was very successful, and was probably the *First Part of Henry VI*. In the autumn of 1592 Robert Greene, the best known of the professional writers, as he was dying wrote a letter to three fellow writers in which he warned them against the ingratitude of players in general, and in particular against an 'upstart crow' who 'supposes he is as much able to bombast out a blank verse as the best of you: and being an absolute Johannes Factotum is in his own conceit the only

Shake-scene in a country.' This is the first reference to Shakespeare, and the whole passage suggests that Shakespeare had become suddenly famous as a playwright. At this time Shakespeare was brought into touch with Edward Alleyne the great tragedian, and Christopher Marlowe, whose thundering parts of Tamburlaine, the Jew of Malta and Dr Faustus Alleyne was acting, as well as Hieronimo, the hero of Kyd's *Spanish Tragedy*, the most famous of all Elizabethan plays.

In April, 1593, Shakespeare published his poem *Venus and Adonis*, which was dedicated to the young Earl of Southampton : it was a great and lasting success, and was reprinted nine times in the next few years. In May, 1594, his second poem, *The Rape of Lucrece*, was also dedicated to Southampton.

There was little playing in 1593, for the theatres were shut during a severe outbreak of the plague; but in the autumn of 1594, when the plague ceased, the playing companies were re-organized, and Shakespeare became a sharer in the Lord Chamberlain's company who went to play in the Theatre in Shoreditch. During these months Marlowe and Kyd had died. Shakespeare was thus for a time without a rival. He had already written the three parts of *Henry VI*, *Richard III*, *Titus Andronicus*, *The Two Gentlemen of Verona*, *Love's Labour's Lost*, *The Comedy of Errors*, and *The Taming of the Shrew*. Soon afterwards he wrote the first of his greater plays – *Romeo and Juliet* – and he followed this success in the next three years with *A Midsummer Night's Dream*, *Richard II*, and *The Merchant of Venice*. The two parts of *Henry IV*, introducing Falstaff, the most popular of all his comic characters, were written in 1597–8.

The company left the Theatre in 1597 owing to disputes over a renewal of the ground lease, and went to play at the

Curtain in the same neighbourhood. The disputes continued throughout 1598, and at Christmas the players settled the matter by demolishing the old Theatre and re-erecting a new playhouse on the South bank of the Thames, near Southwark Cathedral. This playhouse was named the Globe. The expenses of the new building were shared by the chief members of the Company, including Shakespeare, who was now a man of some means. In 1596 he had bought New Place, a large house in the centre of Stratford, for £60, and through his father purchased a coat-of-arms from the Heralds, which was the official recognition that he and his family were gentlefolk.

By the summer of 1598 Shakespeare was recognized as the greatest of English dramatists. Booksellers were printing his more popular plays, at times even in pirated or stolen version, and he received a remarkable tribute from a young writer named Francis Meres, in his book *Palladis Tamia*. In a long catalogue of English authors Meres gave Shakespeare more prominence than any other writer, and mentioned by name twelve of his plays.

Shortly before the Globe was opened, Shakespeare had completed the cycle of plays dealing with the whole story of the Wars of the Roses with *Henry V*. It was followed by *As You Like it*, and *Julius Caesar*, the first of the maturer tragedies. In the next three years he wrote *Troylus and Cressida*, *The Merry Wives of Windsor*, *Hamlet* and *Twelfth Night*.

On March 24, 1603, Queen Elizabeth died. The company had often performed before her, but they found her successor a far more enthusiastic patron. One of the first acts of King James was to take over the company and to promote them to be his own servants, so that henceforward they were known as the King's Men. They acted now very frequently at Court, and prospered accordingly. In the early years of the reign Shakespeare wrote the more sombre comedies, *All's Well that Ends Well*, and *Measure for Measure*, which were followed by *Othello*, *Macbeth* and *King Lear*. Then he returned to Roman themes with *Antony and Cleopatra* and *Coriolanus*.

Since 1601 Shakespeare had been writing less, and there were now a number of rival dramatists who were introducing new styles of drama, particularly Ben Jonson (whose first successful comedy, *Every Man in his Humour*, was acted by Shakespeare's company in 1598), Chapman, Dekker, Marston, and Beaumont and Fletcher who began to write in 1607. In 1608 the King's Men acquired a second playhouse, an indoor private theatre in the fashionable quarter of the Blackfriars. At private theatres, plays were performed indoors; the prices charged were higher than in the public playhouses, and the audience consequently was more select. Shakespeare seems to have retired from the stage about this time: his name does not occur in the various lists of players after 1607. Henceforward he lived for the most part at Stratford where he was regarded as one of the most important citizens. He still wrote a few plays, and he tried his hand at the new form of tragi-comedy – a play with tragic incidents but a happy ending – which Beaumont and Fletcher had popularized. He wrote four of these – *Pericles*, *Cymbeline*, *The Winter's Tale* and *The Tempest*, which was acted at Court in 1611. For the last four years of his life he lived in retirement. His son Hamnet had died in 1596: his two daughters were now married. Shakespeare died at Stratford upon Avon on April 23, 1616, and was buried in the chancel of the church, before the high altar. Shortly afterwards a memorial which still exists, with a portrait bust, was set up on the North wall. His wife survived him.

When Shakespeare died fourteen of his plays had been separately published in Quarto booklets. In 1623 his surviving fellow actors, John Heming and Henry Condell, with the co-operation of a number of printers, published a collected edition of thirty-six plays in one Folio volume, with an engraved portrait, memorial verses by Ben Jonson and others, and an Epistle to the Reader in which Heming and Condell make the interesting note that Shakespeare's 'hand and mind went together, and what he thought, he uttered with that easiness that we have scarce received from him a blot in his papers.'

The plays as printed in the Quartos or the Folio differ considerably from the usual modern text. They are often not divided into scenes, and sometimes not even into acts. Nor are there place-headings at the beginning of each scene, because in the Elizabethan theatre there was no scenery. They are carelessly printed and the spelling is erratic.

## THE ELIZABETHAN THEATRE

Although plays of one sort and another had been acted for many generations, no permanent playhouse was erected in England until 1576. In the 1570's the Lord Mayor and Aldermen of the City of London and the players were constantly at variance. As a result James Burbage, then the leader of the great Earl of Leicester's players, decided that he would erect a playhouse outside the jurisdiction of the Lord Mayor, where the players would no longer be hindered by the authorities. Accordingly in 1576 he built the Theatre in Shoreditch, at that time a suburb of London. The experiment was successful, and by 1592 there were two more playhouses in London, the Curtain (also in Shore-ditch), and the Rose on the south bank of the river, near Southwark Cathedral.

Elizabethan players were accustomed to act on a variety of stages; in the great hall of a nobleman's house, or one of the Queen's palaces, in town halls and in yards, as well as their own theatre.

The public playhouse for which most of Shakespeare's plays were written was a small and intimate affair. The outside measurement of the Fortune Theatre, which was built in 1600 to rival the new Globe, was but eighty feet square. Playhouses were usually circular or octagonal, with three tiers of galleries looking down upon the yard or pit, which was open to the sky. The stage jutted out into the yard so that the actors came forward into the midst of their audience.

Over the stage there was a roof, and on either side doors by which the characters entered or disappeared. Over the back of the stage ran a gallery or upper stage which was used whenever an upper scene was needed, as when Romeo climbs up to Juliet's bedroom, or the citizens of Angiers address King John from the walls. The space beneath this upper stage was known as the tiring house; it was concealed from the audience by a curtain which would be drawn back to reveal an inner stage, for such scenes as the witches' cave in *Macbeth*, Prospero's cell, or Juliet's tomb.

There was no general curtain concealing the whole stage, so that all scenes on the main stage began with an entrance and ended with an exit. Thus in tragedies the dead must be carried away. There was no scenery, and therefore no limit to the number of scenes, for a scene came to an end when the characters left the stage. When it was necessary for the exact locality of a scene to be known, then Shakespeare

**THE GLOBE THEATRE**
*Wood-engraving by R. J. Beedham after a reconstruction by J. C. Adams*

indicated it in the dialogue; otherwise a simple property or a garment was sufficient; a chair or stool showed an indoor scene, a man wearing riding boots was a messenger, a king wearing armour was on the battlefield, or the like. Such simplicity was on the whole an advantage; the spectator was not distracted by the setting and Shakespeare was able to use as many scenes as he wished. The action passed by very quickly; a play of 2500 lines of verse could be acted in two hours. Moreover, since the actor was so close to his audience, the slightest subtlety of voice and gesture was easily appreciated.

The company was a 'Fellowship of Players', who were all partners and sharers. There were usually ten to fifteen full members, with three or four boys, and some paid servants. Shakespeare had therefore to write for his team. The chief actor in the company was Richard Burbage, who first distinguished himself as Richard III; for him Shakespeare wrote his great tragic parts. An important member of the company was the clown or low comedian. From 1594 to 1600 the company's clown was Will Kemp; he was succeeded by Robert Armin. No women were allowed to appear on the stage, and all women's parts were taken by boys.

# AS YOU LIKE IT

*As You Like It* was written before the summer of 1600, and probably in 1599. In the *Stationers' Register* there is a casual note, dated 4th August [1600], that four plays were 'to be staied', i.e. not printed; they were *As You Like It*, *Henry the Fifth*, *Every Man in his Humour*, and *Much Ado about Nothing*. There is also in the play itself a pointed quotation from Marlowe's *Hero and Leander*, which was first published in 1598:

> 'Dead shepherd, now I find thy saw of might:
> Whoever lov'd that lov'd not at first sight.'

The play was probably one of the first new plays to be produced by the Lord Chamberlain's Players in their new playhouse, the Globe, which was first opened about July, 1599.

*As You Like It* thus came out at a time of considerable excitement both for playgoers and the general public. The Earl of Essex had recently gone over to Ireland with a large army to put an end to the rebellion, but from the reports and rumours which were coming back to London matters were clearly going wrong. It was a time of general uneasiness, when cynics expressed themselves freely. In the previous September the Company had produced at the Curtain Theatre Ben Jonson's first successful comedy *Every Man in his Humour*, in which Shakespeare took a part. That play was a great success because it gave an expression to certain prevalent moods which were then coming to the surface. In the late 1590's there was a growing interest in the study of human behaviour as exemplified in certain psychological

types, or 'humours' as the phrase went, and particularly in
the 'melancholic humour'. This interest was first shown in
a succession of satires which began to be published in 1597.
There were a number of these books of satire in the next
two years; but in June, 1599, the Privy Council, uneasily
realising that the satirists were becoming too critical of
great persons, ordered seven volumes of satires to be seized,
and the available copies burnt, and other offending books
to be suppressed – an event to which Celia apparently
refers in the remark:

'– since the little wit that fools have was silenced, the
little foolery that wise men have makes a great show.'

Jonson in *Every Man in his Humour* had translated these
satirical types into drama, for the essence of the comedy of
'humours' was that it displayed typical fools acting according to their humours. Shakespeare was never an imitator
of Jonson, but in *As You Like It* he created one 'humour'
character in the melancholy Jaques.

The story of *As You Like It* came from a novel written by
Thomas Lodge on a voyage to the Canaries, and published
in 1590. It was called *Rosalynde*, and was the most popular
of all the tales of pastoral and romantic adventures which
were then the fashion. *Rosalynde* went into its fourth edition
in 1598, and was therefore well known to Shakespeare's
audience, who would recognize both the similarities and
the differences between the play and the novel. Shakespeare
followed the story fairly closely in the main plot of *As You
Like It*, though he changed some of the names and added
some notable characters of his own. Lodge provided him
with a banished Duke (called Gerismond), Saladyne and
Rosader (whom Shakespeare renamed Oliver and Orlan-

do), Rosalynde and Alinda (Celia), the faithful old Adam
Spencer, Phoebe and her swain Montanus (Silvius). Shakespeare's own characters, for which Lodge gave no sugges-
tion, were Touchstone and Jaques, William and Audrey.
Lodge's story ended a little grimly with the death of the
usurping Duke in battle; Shakespeare, with less probability,
made him a convert to the religious life.

*Rosalynde* was written in that peculiar style which Lyly
had made popular in *Euphues* (first published in 1578). Indeed, to attract the reader and to acknowledge the imitation,
the book had the sub-title 'Euphues' golden Legacy found
after his death in his Cell at Silexedra: Bequeathed to
Philautus' Sons, nursed up with their Father in England'.

Shakespeare, by this time, had little use for this artificial
style, which had become comic to a younger generation of
readers. He rewrote the dialogue entirely. The passage, for
an example, between Rosalind (disguised as Ganymede)
and Phebe, disdainfully scorning her lover (see p. 79, l. 16),
had appeared in *Rosalynde* thus:


'Ganymede, overhearing all these passions of Montanus,
could not brook the cruelty of Phoebe, but starting from
behind the bush said: And if, damsel, you fled from me, I
would transform you as Daphne to a bay, and then in con-
tempt trample your branches under my feet. Phoebe at this
sudden reply was amazed, especially when she saw so fair
a swain as Ganymede; blushing therefore, she would have
been gone, but that he held her by the hand, and prosecuted
his reply thus: What, shepherdess, so fair and so cruel?
Disdain beseems not cottages, nor coyness maids; for either
they be condemned to be too proud, or too froward. Take
heed, fair nymph, that in despising love, you be not over-
reached with love, and in shaking off all, shape yourself to

your own shadow, and so with Narcissus prove passionate
and yet unpitied. Oft have I heard, and sometime have I
seen, high disdain turned to hot desires. Because thou art
beautiful be not so coy: as there is nothing more fair, so
there is nothing more fading; as momentary as the shadows
which grows from a cloudy sun. Such (my fair shepherdess)
as disdain in youth desire in age, and then are they hated in
the winter, that might have been loved in the prime. A
wrinkled maid is like to a parched rose, that is cast up in
coffers to please the smell, not worn in the hand to content
the eye. There is no folly in love to had I wist, and therefore
be ruled by me. Love while thou art young, lest thou be
disdained when thou art old. Beauty nor time cannot be
recalled, and if thou love, like of Montanus; for if his
desires are many, so his deserts are great.'

A brief comparison with *Rosalynde* will show that to
some extent Shakespeare's version in the story is satirical.
Lodge's nymphs and swains are serious in their protesta-
tions; Shakespeare added the Clown Touchstone to be a
cynical and sophisticated commentator whenever the forest
lovers become sentimental. Moreover, by introducing into
the Forest of Arden two real yokels, William and Audrey,
he provided a comic contrast to the pretty ladies and gentlemen who were playing at shepherdesses and foresters.

*As You Like It* was not separately published: it appeared
first in the Folio in 1623. The text is well printed, and the
original punctuation in some speeches – especially those of
Jaques – is subtle and delicate.

The Folio text has its own peculiarities. It differs from
modern usage in several ways, particularly in spelling,
punctuation, and use of capitals. The modern custom is to
punctuate according to syntax; Elizabethan punctuation

was intended as a guide for recitation or reading aloud and should therefore be regarded. Capital letters were used very freely. A modern editor is in some difficulty; the 'accepted text' (which was the work of editors of the eighteenth and nineteenth centuries) is some way from Shakespeare's own text. On the other hand, to reprint the Folio as it stands would annoy most readers who are not scholars. The present text is a compromise. It follows the Folio closely. Spelling is modernized, but the original arrangement and punctuation (which 'points' the text for reading aloud) have been left, except where they seemed definitely wrong. A few emendations generally accepted by editors have been kept. The reader who is used to an 'accepted text' may thus find certain unfamiliarities, but the text itself is nearer to that used in Shakespeare's own playhouse.

# As You Like It

# THE ACTORS' NAMES

DUKE, living in banishment
FREDERICK, his brother, and usurper of his dominions
AMIENS  
JAQUES } lords attending on the banished Duke
LE BEAU, a courtier attending upon Frederick
CHARLES, wrestler to Frederick
OLIVER  
SECOND BROTHER } sons of Sir Rowland de Boys  
ORLANDO
ADAM  
DENNIS } servants to Oliver
TOUCHSTONE, a clown
SIR OLIVER MAR-TEXT, a minister
CORIN  
SYLVIUS } shepherds
WILLIAM, a country fellow, in love with Audrey
A person representing Hymen

ROSALIND, daughter to the banished Duke
CELIA, daughter to Frederick
PHEBE, a shepherdess
AUDREY, a country wench

# I.1

*Enter Orlando and Adam.*

ORLANDO: As I remember Adam, it was upon this fashion
bequeathed me by will, but poor a thousand crowns,
and, as thou sayest, charged my brother on his blessing  5
to breed me well: and there begins my sadness: my
brother Jaques he keeps at school, and report speaks gol-
denly of his profit: for my part, he keeps me rustically
at home, or, to speak more properly, stays me here at
home unkept: for call you that keeping for a gentleman  10
of my birth, that differs not from the stalling of an ox?
His horses are bred better, for besides that they are fair
with their feeding, they are taught their manage, and to
that end riders dearly hir'd: but I, his brother, gain nothing under him but growth, for the which his animals on  15
his dunghills are as much bound to him as I: besides this
nothing that he so plentifully gives me, the something
that nature gave me, his countenance seems to take from
me: he lets me feed with his hinds, bars me the place of a
brother, and as much as in him lies, mines my gentility  20
with my education. This is it Adam, that grieves me,
and the spirit of my father, which I think is within me,
begins to mutiny against this servitude. I will no longer
endure it, though yet I know no wise remedy how to
avoid it.  25

*Enter Oliver.*

ADAM: Yonder comes my master, your brother.

ORLANDO: Go apart Adam, and thou shalt hear how he
will shake me up.

OLIVER: Now sir what make you here?  30

ORLANDO: Nothing: I am not taught to make any thing.

OLIVER: What mar you then sir?

ORLANDO: Marry sir, I am helping you to mar that which God made, a poor unworthy brother of yours with idleness.

OLIVER: Marry sir be better employed, and be naught awhile.

ORLANDO: Shall I keep your hogs, and eat husks with them? What prodigal portion have I spent, that I should come to such penury?

OLIVER: Know you where you are sir?

ORLANDO: O sir, very well: here in your orchard.

OLIVER: Know you before whom sir?

ORLANDO: Ay, better than him I am before knows me: I know you are my eldest brother, and, in the gentle condition of blood you should so know me: the courtesy of nations allows you my better, in that you are the first-born, but the same tradition takes not away my blood, were there twenty brothers betwixt us: I have as much of my father in me, as you, albeit I confess your coming before me is nearer to his reverence.

OLIVER: What boy.

ORLANDO: Come, come elder brother, you are too young in this.

OLIVER: Wilt thou lay hands on me villain?

ORLANDO: I am no villain: I am the youngest son of Sir Rowland de Boys, he was my father, and he is thrice a villain that says such a father begot villains: wert thou not my brother, I would not take this hand from thy throat, till this other hand pulled out thy tongue for saying so: thou hast railed on thyself.

ADAM: Sweet masters be patient; for your father's remembrance, be at accord.

OLIVER: Let me go I say.

ORLANDO: I will not till I please: you shall hear me: my
  father charg'd you in his will to give me good education:
  you have train'd me like a peasant, obscuring and hiding
  from me all gentlemanlike qualities: the spirit of my      5
  father grows strong in me, and I will no longer endure
  it: therefore allow me such exercises as may become a
  gentleman, or give me the poor allottery my father lett
  me by testament, with that I will go buy my fortunes.

OLIVER: And what wilt thou do? beg when that is spent?     10
  Well sir, get you in. I will not long be troubled with
  you: you shall have some part of your will; I pray you
  leave me.

ORLANDO: I will no further offend you, than becomes me
  for my good.                                               15

OLIVER: Get you with him, you old dog.

ADAM: Is old dog my reward? Most true, I have lost my
  teeth in your service: God be with my old master, he
  would not have spoke such a word.

             *Exeunt Orlando and Adam.*                     20

OLIVER: Is it even so, begin you to grow upon me? I will
  physic your rankness, and yet give no thousand crowns
  neither: holla Dennis.

             *Enter Dennis.*

DENNIS: Calls your worship?                                 25

OLIVER: Was not Charles the Duke's wrestler here to
  speak with me?

DENNIS: So please you, he is here at the door, and impor-
  tunes access to you.

OLIVER: Call him in: [*Exit Dennis*] 'twill be a good way;  30
  and to-morrow the wrestling is.

             *Enter Charles.*

CHARLES: Good morrow to your worship.

OLIVER: Good Monsieur Charles: what's the new news at the new Court?

CHARLES; There's no news at the Court sir, but the old news: that is, the old Duke is banished by his younger brother the new Duke, and three or four loving Lords have put themselves into voluntary exile with him, whose lands and revenues enrich the new Duke; therefore he gives them good leave to wander.

OLIVER: Can you tell me if Rosalind the Duke's daughter be banished with her father?

CHARLES: O no; for the Duke's daughter her cousin so loves her, being ever from their cradles bred together, that she would have followed her exile, or have died to stay behind her; she is at the Court, and no less beloved of her uncle, than his own daughter, and never two Ladies loved as they do.

OLIVER: Where will the old Duke live?

CHARLES: They say he is already in the Forest of Arden, and a many merry men with him: and there they live like the old Robin Hood of England: they say many young gentlemen flock to him every day, and fleet the time carelessly as they did in the golden world.

OLIVER: What, you wrestle to-morrow before the new Duke?

CHARLES: Marry do I sir: and I came to acquaint you with a matter: I am given sir, secretly to understand, that your younger brother Orlando hath a disposition to come in disguis'd against me to try a fall: to-morrow sir, I wrestle for my credit, and he that escapes me without some broken limb, shall acquit him well: your brother is but young and tender, and for your love I would be loath to foil him, as I must for my own honour if he come in: therefore out of my love to you, I came hither to acquaint you withal, that either you might stay him from his intendment, or brook such disgrace well as he shall run into, in that it is a thing of his own search, and altogether against my will.

OLIVER: Charles, I thank thee for thy love to me, which 5 thou shalt find I will most kindly requite: I had myself notice of my brother's purpose herein, and have by underhand means laboured to dissuade him from it; but he is resolute. I'll tell thee Charles, it is the stubbornest young fellow of France, full of ambition, an envious 10 emulator of every man's good parts, a secret and villainous contriver against me his natural brother: therefore use thy discretion, I had as lief thou didst break his neck as his finger. And thou wert best look to't; for if thou dost him any slight disgrace, or if he do not mightily grace 15 himself on thee, he will practise against thee by poison, entrap thee by some treacherous device, and never leave thee till he hath ta'en thy life by some indirect means or other: for I assure thee, and almost with tears I speak it, there is not one so young, and so villainous this day liv- 20 ing. I speak but brotherly of him, but should I anatomize him to thee, as he is, I must blush, and weep, and thou must look pale and wonder.

CHARLES: I am heartily glad I came hither to you: if he come to-morrow, I'll give him his payment: if ever he 25 go alone again, I'll never wrestle for prize more: and so God keep your worship.

*Exit Charles.*

OLIVER: Farewell good Charles. Now will I stir this game-ster: I hope I shall see an end of him; for my soul, yet I 30 know not why, hates nothing more than he: yet he's gentle, never school'd, and yet learned, full of noble device, of all sorts enchantingly beloved, and indeed so

much in the heart of the world, and especially of my own people, who best know him, that I am altogether misprised: but it shall not be so long, this wrestler shall clear all: nothing remains, but that I kindle the boy
5 thither, which now I'll go about.

*Exit.*

# I. 2

*Enter Rosalind and Celia.*

CELIA: I pray thee Rosalind, sweet my coz, be merry.
10 ROSALIND: Dear Celia; I show more mirth than I am mistress of, and would you yet were merrier: unless you could teach me to forget a banished father, you must not learn me how to remember any extraordinary pleasure.

CELIA: Herein I see thou lov'st me not with the full weight
15 that I love thee; if my uncle thy banished father had banished thy uncle the Duke my father, so thou hadst been still with me, I could have taught my love to take thy father for mine; so would'st thou, if the truth of thy love to me were so righteously temper'd, as mine is to
20 thee.

ROSALIND: Well, I will forget the condition of my estate, to rejoice in yours.

CELIA: You know my father hath no child, but I, nor none is like to have; and truly when he dies, thou shalt be his
25 heir; for what he hath taken away from thy father perforce, I will render thee again in affection: by mine honour I will, and when I break that oath, let me turn monster: therefore my sweet Rose, my dear Rose, be merry.

30 ROSALIND: From henceforth I will coz, and devise sports: let me see, what think you of falling in love?

CELIA: Marry I prithee do, to make sport withal: but love no man in good earnest, nor no further in sport neither, than with safety of a pure blush, thou mayst in honour come off again.

ROSALIND: What shall be our sport then? 5

CELIA: Let us sit and mock the good housewife Fortune from her wheel, that her gifts may henceforth be bestowed equally.

ROSALIND: I would we could do so: for her benefits are mightily misplaced, and the bountiful blind woman doth 10 most mistake in her gifts to women.

CELIA: 'Tis true, for those that she makes fair, she scarce makes honest, and those that she makes honest, she makes very ill-favouredly.

ROSALIND: Nay now thou goest from Fortune's office to 15 Nature's: Fortune reigns in gifts of the world, not in the lineaments of Nature.

*Enter Clown.*

CELIA: No; when Nature hath made a fair creature, may she not by Fortune fall into the fire? Though Nature 20 hath given us wit to flout at Fortune, hath not Fortune sent in this fool to cut off the argument?

ROSALIND: Indeed there is Fortune too hard for Nature, when Fortune makes Nature's natural, the cutter-off of Nature's wit. 25

CELIA: Peradventure this is not Fortune's work neither, but Nature's who perceiveth our natural wits too dull to reason of such goddesses, and hath sent this natural for our whetstone; for always the dulness of the fool is the whetstone of the wits. How now wit, whither wander 30 you?

TOUCHSTONE: Mistress, you must come away to your father.

CELIA: Were you made the messenger?

TOUCHSTONE: No by mine honour, but I was bid to come for you.

ROSALIND: Where learned you that oath fool?

5 TOUCHSTONE: Of a certain knight, that swore by his honour they were good pancakes, and swore by his honour the mustard was naught: now I'll stand to it, the pancakes were naught, and the mustard was good, and yet was not the knight forsworn.

10 CELIA: How prove you that in the great heap of your knowledge?

ROSALIND: Ay marry, now unmuzzle your wisdom.

TOUCHSTONE: Stand you both forth now: stroke your chins, and swear by your beards that I am a knave

15 CELIA: By our beards (if we had them) thou art.

TOUCHSTONE: By my knavery (if I had it) then I were: but if you swear by that that is not, you are not forsworn: no more was this knight swearing by his honour, for he never had any; or if he had, he had sworn it away,

20 before ever he saw those pancakes, or that mustard.

CELIA: Prithee, who is't that thou mean'st?

TOUCHSTONE: One that old Frederick your father loves.

ROSALIND: My father's love is enough to honour him enough; speak no more of him, you'll be whipt for

25 taxation one of these days.

TOUCHSTONE: The more pity that fools may not speak wisely, what wise men do foolishly.

CELIA: By my troth thou sayest true: for, since the little wit that fools have was silenced, the little foolery that

30 wise men have makes a great show; here comes Monsieur Le Beau.

*Enter Le Beau.*

ROSALIND: With his mouth full of news.

CELIA: Which he will put on us, as pigeons feed their young.

ROSALIND: Then shall we be news-cramm'd.

CELIA: All the better: we shall be the more marketable. *Bon jour Monsieur Le Beau*, what's the news? 5

LE BEAU: Fair Princess, you have lost much good sport.

CELIA: Sport: of what colour?

LE BEAU: What colour Madam? How shall I answer you?

ROSALIND: As wit and fortune will. 10

TOUCHSTONE: Or as the Destinies decrees.

CELIA: Well said, that was laid on with a trowel.

TOUCHSTONE: Nay, if I keep not my rank –

ROSALIND: Thou losest thy old smell.

LE BEAU: You amaze me Ladies: I would have told you 15 of good wrestling, which you have lost the sight of.

ROSALIND: Yet tell us the manner of the wrestling.

LE BEAU: I will tell you the beginning: and if it please your Ladyships, you may see the end, for the best is yet to do, and here where you are, they are coming to per- 20 form it.

CELIA: Well, the beginning that is dead and buried.

LE BEAU: There comes an old man, and his three sons –

CELIA: I could match this beginning with an old tale.

LE BEAU: Three proper young men, of excellent growth 25 and presence.

ROSALIND: With bills on their necks: Be it known unto all men by these presents.

LE BEAU: The eldest of the three, wrestled with Charles the Duke's wrestler, which Charles in a moment threw 30 him, and broke three of his ribs, that there is little hope of life in him: so he serv'd the second, and so the third: yonder they lie, the poor old man their father, making such pitiful dole over them, that all the beholders take his part with weeping.

ROSALIND: Alas.

TOUCHSTONE: But what is the sport Monsieur, that the Ladies have lost?

LE BEAU: Why this that I speak of.

TOUCHSTONE: Thus men may grow wiser every day. It is the first time that ever I heard breaking of ribs was sport for Ladies.

CELIA: Or I, I promise thee.

ROSALIND: But is there any else longs to see this broken music in his sides? Is there yet another dotes upon rib-breaking? Shall we see this wrestling cousin?

LE BEAU: You must if you stay here, for here is the place appointed for the wrestling, and they are ready to perform it.

CELIA: Yonder sure they are coming. Let us now stay and see it.

*Flourish. Enter Duke, Lords, Orlando, Charles and*
*Attendants.*

DUKE: Come on, since the youth will not be entreated, his own peril on his forwardness.

ROSALIND: Is yonder the man?

LE BEAU: Even he, Madam.

CELIA: Alas, he is too young: yet he looks successfully.

DUKE: How now daughter, and cousin: are you crept hither to see the wrestling?

ROSALIND: Ay my Liege, so please you give us leave.

DUKE: You will take little delight in it, I can tell you, there is such odds in the man: in pity of the challenger's youth, I would fain dissuade him, but he will not be entreated. Speak to him Ladies, see if you can move him.

CELIA: Call him hither good Monsieur Le Beau.

DUKE: Do so: I'll not be by.

LEBEAU: Monsieur the challenger, the Princess calls for you.

ORLANDO: I attend them with all respect and duty.

ROSALIND: Young man, have you challeng'd Charles the
wrestler?                                                                            5

ORLANDO: No fair Princess; he is the general challenger;
I come but in as others do, to try with him the strength
of my youth.

CELIA: Young gentleman, your spirits are too bold for
your years: you have seen cruel proof of this man's   10
strength, if you saw yourself with your eyes, or knew
yourself with your judgement, the fear of your adventure would counsel you to a more equal enterprise. We
pray you for your own sake to embrace your own safety,
and give over this attempt.                                                 15

ROSALIND: Do young sir, your reputation shall not therefore be misprised: we will make it our suit to the Duke,
that the wrestling might not go forward.

ORLANDO: I beseech you, punish me not with your hard
thoughts, wherein I confess me much guilty to deny so   20
fair and excellent Ladies any thing. But let your fair eyes,
and gentle wishes go with me to my trial; wherein if I
be foil'd, there is but one sham'd that was never gracious;
if kill'd, but one dead that is willing to be so: I shall do
my friends no wrong, for I have none to lament me:   25
the world no injury, for in it I have nothing: only in
the world I fill up a place, which may be better supplied,
when I have made it empty.

ROSALIND: The little strength that I have, I would it were
with you.                                                                             30

CELIA: And mine to eke out hers.

ROSALIND: Fare you well: pray heaven I be deceiv'd in
you.

CELIA: Your heart's desires be with you.

CHARLES: Come, where is this young gallant, that is so desirous to lie with his mother earth?

ORLANDO: Ready sir, but his will hath in it a more mod-
5 est working.

DUKE: You shall try but one fall.

CHARLES: No, I warrant your Grace you shall not entreat him to a second, that have so mightily persuaded him from a first.

10 ORLANDO: You mean to mock me after: you should not have mock'd me before: but come your ways.

ROSALIND: Now Hercules be thy speed young man.

CELIA: I would I were invisible, to catch the strong fellow by the leg.

15                          *They wrestle.*

ROSALIND: O excellent young man.

CELIA: If I had a thunderbolt in mine eye, I can tell who should down.

                         *Shout.*

20 DUKE: No more, no more.

ORLANDO: Yes, I beseech your Grace, I am not yet well breath'd.

DUKE: How dost thou Charles?

LE BEAU: He cannot speak my Lord.

25 DUKE: Bear him away: what is thy name young man?

ORLANDO: Orlando my Liege, the youngest son of Sir Rowland de Boys.

DUKE: I would thou hadst been son to some man else,
The world esteem'd thy father honourable,
30 But I did find him still mine enemy:
Thou shouldst have better pleas'd me with this deed,
Hadst thou descended from another house:
But fair thee well, thou art a gallant youth,

I would thou hadst told me of another father.
> *Exeunt Duke, &c.*

CELIA: Were I my father, coz, would I do this?

ORLANDO: I am more proud to be Sir Rowland's son,
His youngest son, and would not change that calling      5
To be adopted heir to Frederick.

ROSALIND: My father lov'd Sir Rowland as his soul,
And all the world was of my father's mind:
Had I before known this young man his son,
I should have given him tears unto entreaties,      10
Ere he should thus have ventur'd.

CELIA: Gentle cousin,
Let us go thank him, and encourage him:
My father's rough and envious disposition
Sticks me at heart: sir, you have well deserv'd:      15
If you do keep your promises in love,
But justly as you have exceeded all promise,
Your mistress shall be happy.

ROSALIND: Gentleman,
Wear this for me: one out of suits with fortune      20
That could give more, but that her hand lacks means.
Shall we go coz?

CELIA: Ay: fare you well fair gentleman.

ORLANDO: Can I not say, I thank you? My better parts
Are all thrown down, and that which here stands up      25
Is but a quintain, a mere lifeless block.

ROSALIND: He calls us back: my pride fell with my fortunes,
I'll ask him what he would: did you call sir?
Sir, you have wrestled well, and overthrown
More than your enemies.      30

CELIA: Will you go coz?

ROSALIND: Have with you: fare you well.
> *Exeunt Rosalind and Celia.*

ORLANDO: What passion hangs these weights upon my
    tongue?
    I cannot speak to her, yet she urg'd conference.
               *Enter Le Beau.*
5    O poor Orlando! thou art overthrown
    Or Charles, or something weaker masters thee.
  LE BEAU: Good sir, I do in friendship counsel you
    To leave this place; albeit you have deserv'd
    High commendation, true applause, and love;
10    Yet such is now the Duke's condition,
    That he misconsters all that you have done:
    The Duke is humorous, what he is indeed
    More suits you to conceive, than I to speak of.
  ORLANDO: I thank you sir; and pray you tell me this,
15    Which of the two was daughter of the Duke,
    That here was at the wrestling?
  LE BEAU: Neither his daughter, if we judge by manners,
    But yet indeed the taller is his daughter,
    The other is daughter to the banish'd Duke,
20    And here detain'd by her usurping uncle
    To keep his daughter company, whose loves
    Are dearer than the natural bond of sisters:
    But I can tell you, that of late this Duke
    Hath ta'en displeasure 'gainst his gentle niece,
25    Grounded upon no other argument,
    But that the people praise her for her virtues,
    And pity her, for her good father's sake;
    And on my life his malice 'gainst the Lady
    Will suddenly break forth: sir, fare you well,
30    Hereinafter in a better world than this,
    I shall desire more love and knowledge of you.
  ORLANDO: I rest much bounden to you: fare you well.
               *Exit Le Beau.*

Thus must I from the smoke into the smother,
From tyrant Duke, unto a tyrant brother.
But heavenly Rosalind.

*Exit.*

# I. 3                                                                    5

*Enter Celia and Rosalind.*

CELIA: Why cousin, why Rosalind: Cupid have mercy,
not a word?

ROSALIND: Not one to throw at a dog.

CELIA: No, thy words are too precious to be cast away  10
upon curs, throw some of them at me; come lame me
with reasons.

ROSALIND: Then there were two cousins laid up, when
the one should be lam'd with reasons, and the other mad
without any.                                                            15

CELIA: But is all this for your father?

ROSALIND: No, some of it is for my child's father: Oh
how full of briers is this working-day world.

CELIA: They are but burs, cousin, thrown upon thee in
holiday foolery; if we walk not in the trodden paths  20
our very petticoats will catch them.

ROSALIND: I could shake them off my coat, these burs are
in my heart.

CELIA: Hem them away.

ROSALIND: I would try if I could cry hem, and have him.  25

CELIA: Come, come, wrestle with thy affections.

ROSALIND: O they take the part of a better wrestler than
myself.

CELIA: O, a good wish upon you: you will try in time in
despite of a fall: but turning these jests out of service,  30
let us talk in good earnest: is it possible on such a sudden,

you should fall into so strong a liking with old Sir
Rowland's youngest son?

ROSALIND: The Duke my father lov'd his father dearly.

CELIA: Doth it therefore ensue that you should love his
5 son dearly? By this kind of chase, I should hate him, for
my father hated his father dearly; yet I hate not Orlando.

ROSALIND: No faith, hate him not for my sake.

CELIA: Why should I not? doth he not deserve well?

*Enter Duke with Lords.*

10 ROSALIND: Let me love him for that, and do you love
him because I do. Look, here comes the Duke.

CELIA: With his eyes full of anger.

DUKE: Mistress, dispatch you with your safest haste,
And get you from our Court.

15 ROSALIND: Me uncle?

DUKE: You cousin,
Within these ten days if that thou be'st found
So near our public Court as twenty miles,
Thou diest for it.

20 ROSALIND: I do beseech your Grace,
Let me the knowledge of my fault bear with me:
If with myself I hold intelligence,
Or have acquaintance with mine own desires,
If that I do not dream, or be not frantic,
25 As I do trust I am not, then dear uncle,
Never so much as in a thought unborn,
Did I offend your Highness.

DUKE: Thus do all traitors,
If their purgation did consist in words,
30 They are as innocent as grace itself;
Let it suffice thee that I trust thee not.

ROSALIND: Yet your mistrust cannot make me a traitor;
Tell me whereon the likelihoods depends.

DUKE: Thou art thy father's daughter, there's enough.

ROSALIND: So was I when your Highness took his Dukedom,

So was I when your Highness banish'd him;

Treason is not inherited my Lord,                                5

Or if we did derive it from our friends,

What's that to me, my father was no traitor,

Then good my Liege, mistake me not so much,

To think my poverty is treacherous.

CELIA: Dear Sovereign hear me speak.                       10

DUKE: Ay Celia, we stay'd her for your sake,

Else had she with her father rang'd along.

CELIA: I did not then entreat to have her stay,

It was your pleasure, and your own remorse;

I was too young that time to value her,                      15

But now I know her: if she be a traitor,

Why so am I: we still have slept together,

Rose at an instant, learn'd, play'd, eat together,

And whereso'er we went, like Juno's swans,

Still we went coupled and inseparable.                      20

DUKE: She is too subtle for thee, and her smoothness,

Her very silence, and her patience,

Speak to the people, and they pity her:

Thou art a fool, she robs thee of thy name,

And thou wilt show more bright, and seem more vir-  25
tuous

When she is gone: then open not thy lips;

Firm, and irrevocable is my doom,

Which I have pass'd upon her, she is banish'd.

CELIA: Pronounce that sentence then on me my Liege,   30

I cannot live out of her company.

DUKE: You are a fool: you niece provide yourself,

If you outstay the time, upon mine honour,

And in the greatness of my word you die.
*Exeunt Duke &c.*

CELIA: O my poor Rosalind, whither wilt thou go?
Wilt thou change fathers? I will give thee mine:
5   I charge thee be not thou more griev'd than I am.

ROSALIND: I have more cause.

CELIA: Thou hast not cousin,
Prithee be cheerful; know'st thou not the Duke
Hath banish'd me his daughter?

10  ROSALIND: That he hath not.

CELIA: No, hath not? Rosalind lacks then the love
Which teacheth thee that thou and I am one,
Shall we be sunder'd? shall we part sweet girl?
No, let my father seek another heir:
15   Therefore devise with me how we may fly,
Whither to go, and what to bear with us;
And do not seek to take your change upon you,
To bear your griefs yourself, and leave me out:
For by this heaven, now at our sorrows pale,
20   Say what thou canst, I'll go along with thee.

ROSALIND: Why, whither shall we go?

CELIA: To seek my uncle in the Forest of Arden.

ROSALIND: Alas, what danger will it be to us,
Maids as we are, to travel forth so far?
25   Beauty provoketh thieves sooner than gold.

CELIA: I'll put myself in poor and mean attire,
And with a kind of umber smirch my face;
The like do you, so shall we pass along,
And never stir assailants.

30  ROSALIND: Were it not better,
Because that I am more than common tall,
That I did suit me all points like a man,
A gallant curtle-axe upon my thigh,

A boar-spear in my hand, and in my heart
Lie there what hidden woman's fear there will,
We'll have a swashing and a martial outside,
As many other mannish cowards have,
That do outface it with their semblances.                    5

CELIA: What shall I call thee when thou art a man?

ROSALIND: I'll have no worse a name than Jove's own
    page,
And therefore look you call me Ganymede.
But what will you be call'd?                                 10

CELIA: Something that hath a reference to my state:
No longer Celia, but Aliena.

ROSALIND: But cousin, what if we assay'd to steal
The clownish fool out of your father's Court?
Would he not be a comfort to our travel?                     15

CELIA: He'll go along o'er the wide world with me,
Leave me alone to woo him: let's away
And get our jewels and our wealth together,
Devise the fittest time, and safest way
To hide us from pursuit that will be made                    20
After my flight: now go we in content
To liberty, and not to banishment.

*Exeunt.*

# II. 1

*Enter Duke senior, Amiens and two or three Lords like*      25
*foresters.*

DUKE SENIOR: Now my co-mates, and brothers in exile
Hath not old custom made this life more sweet
Than that of painted pomp? Are not these woods
More free from peril than the envious Court?                 30
Here feel we not the penalty of Adam,

The seasons' difference, as the icy fang
And churlish chiding of the winter's wind,
Which when it bites, and blows upon my body
Even till I shrink with cold, I smile, and say
5 This is no flattery: these are counsellors
That feelingly persuade me what I am:
Sweet are the uses of adversity
Which like the toad, ugly and venomous,
Wears yet a precious jewel in his head:
10 And this our life exempt from public haunt,
Finds tongues in trees, books in the running brooks
Sermons in stones, and good in every thing.
AMIENS: I would not change it; happy is your Grace
That can translate the stubbornness of fortune
15 Into so quiet and so sweet a style.
DUKE SENIOR: Come, shall we go and kill us venison?
And yet it irks me the poor dappled fools
Being native burghers of this desert city,
Should in their own confines with forked heads
20 Have their round haunches gor'd.
1 LORD: Indeed my Lord,
The melancholy Jaques grieves at that,
And in that kind swears you do more usurp
Than doth your brother that hath banish'd you:
25 To-day my Lord of Amiens, and myself,
Did steal behind him as he lay along
Under an oak, whose antique root peeps out
Upon the brook that brawls along this wood,
To the which place a poor sequester'd stag
30 That from the hunter's aim had ta'en a hurt,
Did come to languish; and indeed my Lord,
The wretched animal heav'd forth such groans
That their discharge did stretch his leathern coat

Almost to bursting, and the big round tears
Cours'd one another down his innocent nose
In piteous chase: and thus the hairy fool,
Much marked of the melancholy Jaques,
Stood on th' extremest verge of the swift brook,      5
Augmenting it with tears.

DUKE SENIOR: But what said Jaques?
Did he not moralize this spectacle?

1 LORD: O yes, into a thousand similes.
First, for his weeping into the needless stream;      10
Poor deer quoth he, thou mak'st a testament
As worldlings do, giving thy sum of more
To that which had too much: then being there alone.
Left and abandoned of his velvet friend;
'Tis right quoth he, thus misery doth part      15
The flux of company: anon a careless herd
Full of the pasture, jumps along by him
And never stays to greet him: Ay quoth Jaques,
Sweep on you fat and greasy citizens,
'Tis just the fashion; wherefore do you look      20
Upon that poor and broken bankrupt there?
Thus most invectively he pierceth through
The body of the Country, City, Court,
Yea, and of this our life, swearing that we
Are mere usurpers, tyrants, and what's worse,      25
To fright the animals, and to kill them up
In their assign'd and native dwelling-place.

DUKE SENIOR: And did you leave him in this contem-
      plation?

2 LORD: We did my Lord, weeping and commenting      30
Upon the sobbing deer.

DUKE SENIOR: Show me the place,
I love to cope him in these sullen fits,

For then he's full of matter.

1 LORD: I'll bring you to him straight.

*Exeunt.*

## II. 2

*Enter Duke, with Lords.*

DUKE: Can it be possible that no man saw them?
It cannot be, some villains of my Court
Are of consent and sufferance in this.

1 LORD: I cannot hear of any that did see her,
The Ladies her attendants of her chamber
Saw her a-bed, and in the morning early,
They found the bed untreasur'd of their mistress.

2 LORD: My Lord, the roynish clown, at whom so oft,
Your Grace was wont to laugh is also missing.
Hisperia the Princess' gentlewoman,
Confesses that she secretly o'erheard
Your daughter and her cousin much commend
The parts and graces of the wrestler
That did but lately foil the sinewy Charles,
And she believes wherever they are gone
That youth is surely in their company.

DUKE: Send to his brother, fetch that gallant hither,
If he be absent, bring his brother to me,
I'll make him find him: do this suddenly;
And let not search and inquisition quail,
To bring again these foolish runaways.

*Exeunt.*

## II. 3

*Enter Orlando and Adam.*

ORLANDO: Who's there?

ADAM: What my young master, O my gentle master,
O my sweet master, O you memory                                    5
Of old Sir Rowland; why, what make you here?
Why are you virtuous? Why do people love you?
And wherefore are you gentle, strong and valiant?
Why would you be so fond to overcome
The bonny priser of the humorous Duke?                             10
Your praise is come too swiftly home before you.
Know you not master, to some kind of men,
Their graces serve them but as enemies,
No more do yours: your virtues gentle master,
Are sanctified and holy traitors to you;                           15
Oh what a world is this, when what is comely
Envenoms him that bears it?

ORLANDO: Why, what's the matter?

ADAM: O unhappy youth,
Come not within these doors: within this roof                      20
The enemy of all your graces lives
Your brother, no, no brother, yet the son
(Yet not the son, I will not call him son)
Of him I was about to call his father,
Hath heard your praises, and this night he means,                  25
To burn the lodging where you use to lie,
And you within it: if he fail of that
He will have other means to cut you off;
I overheard him: and his practices:
This is no place, this house is but a butchery;                    30
Abhor it, fear it, do not enter it.

ORLANDO: Why, whither Adam wouldst thou have me
   go?
ADAM: No matter whither, so you come not here.
ORLANDO: What, wouldst thou have me go and beg my
5    food,
   Or with a base and boisterous sword enforce
   A thievish living on the common road?
   This I must do, or know not what to do:
   Yet this I will not do, do how I can,
10  I rather will subject me to the malice
   Of a diverted blood, and bloody brother.
ADAM: But do not so: I have five hundred crowns,
   The thrifty hire I saved under your father,
   Which I did store to be my foster-nurse,
15  When service should in my old limbs lie lame,
   And unregarded age in corners thrown,
   Take that, and He that doth the ravens feed,
   Yea providently caters for the sparrow,
   Be comfort to my age: here is the gold,
20  All this I give you, let me be your servant,
   Though I look old, yet I am strong and lusty;
   For in my youth I never did apply.
   Hot, and rebellious liquors in my blood,
   Nor did not with unbashful forehead woo,
25  The means of weakness and debility,
   Therefore my age is as a lusty winter,
   Frosty, but kindly; let me go with you,
   I'll do the service of a younger man
   In all your business and necessities.
30 ORLANDO: O good old man, how well in thee appears
   The constant service of the antique world,
   When service sweat for duty, not for meed:
   Thou art not for the fashion of these times,

Where none will sweat, but for promotion,
And having that do choke their service up,
Even with the having, it is not so with thee:
But poor old man, thou prun'st a rotten tree,
That cannot so much as a blossom yield,                    5
In lieu of all thy pains and husbandry;
But come thy ways, we'll go along together,
And ere we have thy youthful wages spent,
We'll light upon some settled low content.
ADAM: Master go on, and I will follow thee               10
To the last gasp with truth and loyalty,
From seventeen years, till now almost fourscore
Here lived I, but now live here no more.
At seventeen years, many their fortunes seek;
But at fourscore, it is too late a week;                   15
Yet fortune cannot recompense me better
Than to die well, and not my master's debtor.
                    *Exeunt.*

# II. 4

*Enter Rosalind for Ganymede, Celia for Aliena, and*       20
*Clown, alias Touchstone.*

ROSALIND: O Jupiter, how merry are my spirits!
CLOWN: I care not for my spirits, if my legs were not weary.
ROSALIND: I could find in my heart to disgrace my man's
apparel, and to cry like a woman: but I must comfort the   25
weaker vessel, as doublet and hose ought to show itself
courageous to petticoat; therefore courage, good Aliena.
CELIA: I pray you bear with me, I cannot go no further.
CLOWN: For my part, I had rather bear with you, than
bear you; yet I should bear no cross if I did bear you,     30
for I think you have no money in your purse.

ROSALIND: Well, this is the Forest of Arden.

CLOWN: Ay, now am I in Arden, the more fool I; when I was at home I was in a better place, but travellers must be content.

5                      *Enter Corin and Sylvius.*

ROSALIND: Ay, be so good Touchstone: look you, who comes here, a young man and an old in solemn talk.

CORIN: That is the way to make her scorn you still.

SYLVIUS: O Corin, that thou knew'st how I do love her.

10 CORIN: I partly guess: for I have lov'd ere now.

SYLVIUS: No Corin, being old, thou canst not guess,
Though in thy youth thou wast as true a lover
As ever sigh'd upon a midnight pillow:
But if thy love were ever like to mine,
15 As sure I think did never man love so:
How many actions most ridiculous,
Hast thou been drawn to by thy fantasy?

CORIN: Into a thousand that I have forgotten.

SYLVIUS: Oh thou didst then ne'er love so heartily,
20 If thou remember'st not the slightest folly,
That ever love did make thee run into,
Thou hast not lov'd.
Or if thou hast not sat as I do now,
Wearing thy hearer in thy mistress' praise,
25 Thou hast not lov'd.
Or if thou hast not broke from company,
Abruptly as my passion now makes me,
Thou hast not lov'd.
O Phebe, Phebe, Phebe.

30                                *Exit.*

ROSALIND: Alas poor shepherd, searching of thy wound,
I have by hard adventure found mine own.

CLOWN: And I mine: I remember when I was in love, I

broke my sword upon a stone, and bid him take that
for coming a-night to Jane Smile, and I remember the
kissing of her batler, and the cow's dugs that her pretty
chopt hands had milk'd; and I remember the wooing of
a peascod instead of her, from whom I took two cods,   5
and giving her them again, said with weeping tears,
Wear these for my sake: we that are true lovers, run into
strange capers; but as all is mortal in nature, so is all
nature in love, mortal in folly.

ROSALIND: Thou speakest wiser than thou art ware of.   10

CLOWN: Nay, I shall ne'er be ware of mine own wit, till
I break my shins against it.

ROSALIND: Jove, Jove, this shepherd's passion,
Is much upon my fashion.

CLOWN: And mine, but it grows something stale with me.   15

CELIA: I pray you, one of you question yond man,
If he for gold will give us any food,
I faint almost to death.

CLOWN: Holla; you clown.

ROSALIND: Peace fool, he's not thy kinsman.   20

CORIN: Who calls?

CLOWN: Your betters sir.

CORIN: Else are they very wretched.

ROSALIND: Peace I say; good even to you friend.

CORIN: And to you gentle sir, and to you all.   25

ROSALIND: I prithee shepherd, if that love or gold
Can in this desert place buy entertainment,
Bring us where we may rest ourselves, and feed:
Here's a young maid with travel much oppress'd,
And faints for succour.   30

CORIN: Fair sir, I pity her,
And wish for her sake more than for mine own,
My fortunes were more able to relieve her:

But I am shepherd to another man,
And do not shear the fleeces that I graze:
My master is of churlish disposition,
And little recks to find the way to heaven
5    By doing deeds of hospitality.
Besides his cote, his flocks, and bounds of feed
Are now on sale, and at our sheepcote now
By reason of his absence there is nothing
That you will feed on: but what is, come see,
10    And in my voice most welcome shall you be.
ROSALIND: What is he that shall buy his flock and pasture?
CORIN: That young swain that you saw here but erewhile,
That little cares for buying any thing.
ROSALIND: I pray thee, if it stand with honesty,
15    Buy thou the cottage, pasture, and the flock,
And thou shalt have to pay for it of us.
CELIA: And we will mend thy wages: I like this place,
And willingly could waste my time in it.
CORIN: Assuredly the thing is to be sold:
20    Go with me, if you like upon report,
The soil, the profit, and this kind of life,
I will your very faithful feeder be,
And buy it with your gold right suddenly.
            *Exeunt.*


25    # II. 5

*Enter Amiens, Jaques, and others.*
### SONG
AMIENS:        *Under the greenwood tree*
            *Who loves to lie with me,*
30            *And turn his merry note,*
            *Unto the sweet bird's throat:*

*Come hither, come hither, come hither:*
    *Here shall he see no enemy,*
    *But winter and rough weather.*

JAQUES: More, more, I prithee more.

AMIENS: It will make you melancholy Monsieur Jaques. 5

JAQUES: I thank it: more, I prithee more. I can suck melancholy out of a song, as a weasel sucks eggs: more, I prithee more.

AMIENS: My voice is ragged, I know I cannot please you.

JAQUES: I do not desire you to please me, I do desire you 10 to sing: come, more, another stanzo: call you 'em stanzos?

AMIENS: What you will Monsieur Jaques.

JAQUES: Nay, I care not for their names, they owe me nothing. Will you sing? 15

AMIENS: More at your request, than to please myself.

JAQUES: Well then, if ever I thank any man, I'll thank you: but that they call compliment is like th' encounter of two dog-apes. And when a man thanks me heartily, methinks I have given him a penny, and he renders me 20 the beggarly thanks. Come sing; and you that will not hold your tongues.

AMIENS: Well, I'll end the song. Sirs, cover the while, the Duke will drink under this tree; he hath been all this day to look for you. 25

JAQUES: And I have been all this day to avoid him: he is too disputable for my company: I think of as many matters as he, but I give heaven thanks, and make no boast of them. Come, warble, come.

    *Song. All together here.* 30

    *Who doth ambition shun,*
        *And loves to live i' th' sun:*

> *Seeking the food he eats,*
> *And pleas'd with what he gets:*
> *Come hither, come hither, come hither,*
> *Here shall he see, &c.*

5 JAQUES: I'll give you a verse to this note, that I made yes-
terday in despite of my invention.
AMIENS: And I'll sing it.
JAQUES: Thus it goes.

> *If it do come to pass, that any man turn ass:*
10 > *Leaving his wealth and ease,*
> *A stubborn will to please,*
> *Ducdame, ducdame, ducdame:*
> *Here shall he see, gross fools as he,*
> *And if he will come to me.*

15 AMIENS: What's that ducdame?
JAQUES: 'Tis a Greek invocation, to call fools into a circle.
I'll go sleep if I can: if I cannot, I'll rail against all the
first-born of Egypt.
AMIENS: And I'll go see the Duke, his banquet is prepar'd.
20 *Exeunt.*

# II. 6

*Enter Orlando, and Adam.*

ADAM: Dear master, I can go no further: O I die for food.
Here lie I down, and measure out my grave. Farewell
25 kind master.
ORLANDO: Why how now Adam? No greater heart in
thee: live a little, comfort a little, cheer thyself a little.
If this uncouth Forest yield any thing savage, I will either

be food for it, or bring it for food to thee: thy conceit
is nearer death, than thy powers. For my sake be comfortable, hold death awhile at the arm's end: I will here
be with thee presently, and if I bring thee not something
to eat, I will give thee leave to die: but if thou diest before   5
I come, thou art a mocker of my labour. Well said, thou
look'st cheerly, and I'll be with thee quickly: yet thou
liest in the bleak air. Come, I will bear thee to some
shelter, and thou shalt not die for lack of a dinner, if
there live any thing in this desert. Cheerly good Adam.   10
*Exeunt.*

# II. 7

*Enter Duke senior, and Lords like outlaws.*

DUKE SENIOR: I think he be transform'd into a beast,
  For I can no where find him, like a man.   15

1 LORD: My Lord, he is but even now gone hence,
  Here was he merry, hearing of a song.

DUKE SENIOR: If he compact of jars, grow musical,
  We shall have shortly discord in the spheres:
  Go seek him, tell him I would speak with him.   20

*Enter Jaques.*

1 LORD: He saves my labour by his own approach.

DUKE SENIOR: Why how now Monsieur, what a life is
  this
  That your poor friends must woo your company;   25
  What, you look merrily.

JAQUES: A fool, a fool: I met a fool i' th' Forest,
  A motley fool ( a miserable world:)
  As I do live by food, I met a fool,
  Who laid him down, and bask'd him in the sun,   30
  And rail'd on Lady Fortune in good terms,

In good set terms, and yet a motley fool.
Good morrow fool (quoth I:) No sir, quoth he,
Call me not fool, till heaven hath sent me fortune;
And then he drew a dial from his poke,
5 And looking on it, with lack-lustre eye,
Says, very wisely, It is ten o'clock:
Thus we may see (quoth he), how the world wags:
'Tis but an hour ago, since it was nine,
And after one hour more, 'twill be eleven,
10 And so from hour to hour, we ripe, and ripe,
And then from hour to hour, we rot, and rot,
And thereby hangs a tale. When I did hear
The motley fool, thus moral on the time,
My lungs began to crow like Chanticleer,
15 That fools should be so deep-contemplative:
And I did laugh, sans intermission
An hour by his dial. O noble fool,
A worthy fool; motley's the only wear.
DUKE SENIOR: What fool is this?
20 JAQUES: O worthy fool; one that hath been a courtier
And says, if Ladies be but young, and fair,
They have the gift to know it: and in his brain,
Which is as dry as the remainder biscuit
After a voyage, he hath strange places cramm'd
25 With observation, the which he vents
In mangled forms. O that I were a fool,
I am ambitious for a motley coat.
DUKE SENIOR: Thou shalt have one.
JAQUES: It is my only suit,
30 Provided that you weed your better judgements
Of all opinion that grows rank in them,
That I am wise. I must have liberty
Withal, as large a charter as the wind,

To blow on whom I please, for so fools have:
And they that are most galled with my folly,
They most must laugh: and why sir must they so?
The why is plain, as way to parish church:
He, that a fool doth very wisely hit, 5
Doth very foolishly, although he smart,
Not to seem senseless of the bob. If not,
The wise man's folly is anatomiz'd
Even by the squand'ring glances of the fool.
Invest me in my motley: give me leave 10
To speak my mind, and I will through and through
Cleanse the foul body of th' infected world,
If they will patiently receive my medicine.
DUKE SENIOR: Fie on thee, I can tell what thou wouldst
do. 15
JAQUES: What, for a counter, would I do, but good?
DUKE SENIOR: Most mischievous foul sin, in chiding sin:
For thou thyself hast been a libertine,
As sensual as the brutish sting itself,
And all th' embossed sores, and headed evils, 20
That thou with licence of free foot has caught,
Wouldst thou disgorge into the general world.
JAQUES: Why who cried out on pride,
That can therein tax any private party?
Doth it not flow as hugely as the sea, 25
Till that the weary very means do ebb?
What woman in the City do I name,
When that I say the city-woman bears
The cost of Princes on unworthy shoulders?
Who can come in, and say that I mean her, 30
When such a one as she, such is her neighbour?
Or what is he of basest function,
That says his bravery is not on my cost,

Thinking that I mean him, but therein suits
His folly to the mettle of my speech?
There then, how then, what then, let me see wherein
My tongue hath wrong'd him: if it do him right,
5    Then he hath wrong'd himself: if he be free,
Why then my taxing like a wild-goose flies
Unclaim'd of any man. But who comes here?

*Enter Orlando.*

ORLANDO: Forbear, and eat no more.
10  JAQUES: Why I have eat none yet.
ORLANDO: Nor shalt thou, till necessity be serv'd.
JAQUES: Of what kind should this cock come of?
DUKE SENIOR: Art thou thus bolden'd man, by thy distress?
15    Or else a rude despiser of good manners,
That in civility thou seem'st so empty?
ORLANDO: You touch'd my vein at first, the thorny point
Of bare distress, hath ta'en from me the show
Of smooth civility: yet am I inland bred,
20    And know some nurture: but forbear, I say,
He dies that touches any of this fruit,
Till I, and my affairs are answered.
JAQUES: And you will not be answer'd with reason, I
must die.
25  DUKE SENIOR: What would you have?
Your gentleness shall force, more than your force
Move us to gentleness.
ORLANDO: I almost die for food, and let me have it.
DUKE SENIOR: Sit down and feed, and welcome to our
30    table.
ORLANDO: Speak you so gently? Pardon me I pray you,
I thought that all things had been savage here,
And therefore put I on the countenance

Of stern commandment. But whate'er you are
That in this desert inaccessible,
Under the shade of melancholy boughs,
Lose, and neglect the creeping hours of time:
If ever you have look'd on better days:                    5
If ever been where bells have knoll'd to church:
If ever sat at any good man's feast:
If ever from your eyelids wip'd a tear,
And know what 'tis to pity, and be pitied:
Let gentleness my strong enforcement be,                 10
In the which hope, I blush, and hide my sword.

DUKE SENIOR: True it is, that we have seen better days,
And have with holy bell been knoll'd to church,
And sat at good men's feasts, and wip'd our eyes
Of drops, that sacred pity hath engender'd:              15
And therefore sit you down in gentleness,
And take upon command, what help we have
That to your wanting may be minister'd.

ORLANDO: Then but forbear your food a little while:
Whiles (like a doe) I go to find my fawn,                20
And give it food. There is an old poor man,
Who after me, hath many a weary step
Limp'd in pure love: till he be first suffic'd,
Oppress'd with two weak evils, age, and hunger,
I will not touch a bit.                                  25

DUKE SENIOR: Go find him out,
And we will nothing waste till you return.

ORLANDO: I thank ye, and be blest for your good comfort.
                        *Exit.*

DUKE SENIOR: Thou seest, we are not all alone unhappy:   30
This wide and universal theatre
Presents more woeful pageants than the scene
Wherein we play in.

JAQUES: All the world's a stage,
And all the men and women, merely Players;
They have their exits and their entrances,
And one man in his time plays many parts,
5   His Acts being seven ages. At first the infant,
Mewling, and puking in the nurse's arms:
Then, the whining school-boy with his satchel
And shining morning face, creeping like a snail
Unwillingly to school. And then the lover,
10  Sighing like furnace, with a woeful ballad
Made to his mistress' eyebrow. Then, a soldier,
Full of strange oaths, and bearded like the pard,
Jealous in honour, sudden, and quick in quarrel,
Seeking the bubble reputation
15  Even in the cannon's mouth: and then, the justice,
In fair round belly, with good capon lin'd,
With eyes severe, and beard of formal cut,
Full of wise saws, and modern instances,
And so he plays his part. The sixth age shifts
20  Into the lean and slipper'd pantaloon,
With spectacles on nose, and pouch on side,
His youthful hose well sav'd, a world too wide,
For his shrunk shank, and his big manly voice,
Turning again toward childish treble pipes,
25  And whistles in his sound. Last scene of all,
That ends this strange eventful history,
Is second childishness, and mere oblivion,
Sans teeth, sans eyes, sans taste, sans everything.
            *Enter Orlando with Adam.*
30 DUKE SENIOR: Welcome: set down your venerable bur-
      then,
   And let him feed.
   ORLANDO: I thank you most for him.

ADAM: So had you need,
  I scarce can speak to thank you for myself.
DUKE SENIOR: Welcome, fall to: I will not trouble you,
  As yet to question you about your fortunes:
  Give us some music, and good cousin, sing.     5

SONG

    *Blow, blow, thou winter wind,*
  *Thou art not so unkind, as man's ingratitude;*
  *Thy tooth is not so keen, because thou art not seen,*
      *Although thy breath be rude.*     10
  *Heigh-ho, sing heigh-ho, unto the green holly,*
  *Most friendship, is feigning; most loving, mere folly:*
      *Then heigh-ho, the holly,*
        *This life is most jolly.*
  *Freeze, freeze, thou bitter sky that dost not bite so nigh*     15
      *As benefits forgot:*
  *Though thou the waters warp, thy sting is not so sharp,*
      *As friend remember'd not.*
  *Heigh-ho, sing, &c.*

DUKE SENIOR: If that you were the good Sir Rowland's  20
  son,
  As you have whisper'd faithfully you were,
  And as mine eye doth his effigies witness,
  Most truly limn'd, and living in your face,
  Be truly welcome hither: I am the Duke     25
  That lov'd your father; the residue of your fortune,
  Go to my cave, and tell me. Good old man.
  Thou art right welcome, as thy master is:
  Support him by the arm: give me your hand,
  And let me all your fortunes understand.     30

*Exeunt.*

## III. 1

*Enter Duke, Lords, and Oliver.*

DUKE: Not see him since? Sir, sir, that cannot be:
But were I not the better part made mercy,
5    I should not seek an absent argument
Of my revenge, thou present: but look to it,
Find out thy brother whereso'er he is,
Seek him with candle: bring him dead, or living
Within this twelvemonth, or turn thou no more
10    To seek a living in our territory.
Thy lands and all things that thou dost call thine,
Worth seizure, do we seize into our hands,
Till thou canst quit thee by thy brother's mouth,
Of what we think against thee.

15 OLIVER: O that your Highness knew my heart in this:
I never lov'd my brother in my life.

DUKE: More villain thou. Well push him out of doors
And let my officers of such a nature
Make an extent upon his house and lands:
20    Do this expediently, and turn him going.

*Exeunt.*

## III. 2

*Enter Orlando.*

ORLANDO: Hang there my verse, in witness of my love,
25    And thou thrice-crowned Queen of night survey
With thy chaste eye, from thy pale sphere above
Thy huntress' name, that my full life doth sway.
O Rosalind, these trees shall be my books,
And in their barks my thoughts I'll character,

That every eye, which in this forest looks,
Shall see thy virtue witness'd every where.
Run, run, Orlando, carve on every tree,
The fair, the chaste, and unexpressive she.

*Exit.* 5

*Enter Corin and Clown.*

CORIN: And how like you this shepherd's life. Master Touchstone?

CLOWN: Truly shepherd, in respect of itself, it is a good life; but in respect that it is a shepherd's life, it is naught. 10 In respect that it is solitary, I like it very well: but in respect that it is private, it is a very vile life. Now in respect it is in the fields, it pleaseth me well: but in respect it is not in the Court, it is tedious. As it is a spare life (look you) it fits my humour well: but as there is no more 15 plenty in it, it goes much against my stomach. Hast any philosophy in thee shepherd?

CORIN: No more, but that I know the more one sickens, the worse at ease he is: and that he that wants money, means, and content, is without three good friends. That 20 the property of rain is to wet, and fire to burn: that good pasture makes fat sheep: and that a great cause of the night, is lack of the sun: that he that hath learned no wit by Nature, nor Art, may complain of good breeding, or comes of a very dull kindred. 25

CLOWN: Such a one is a natural philosopher: wast ever in Court, shepherd?

CORIN: No truly.

CLOWN: Then thou art damn'd.

CORIN: Nay, I hope. 30

CLOWN: Truly thou art damn'd, like an ill-roasted egg, all on one side.

CORIN: For not being at Court? Your reason.

CLOWN: Why, if thou never wast at Court, thou never sawest good manners: if thou never saw'st good manners, then thy manners must be wicked, and wickedness is sin,
5 and sin is damnation: thou art in a parlous state shepherd.

CORIN: Not a whit Touchstone; those that are good manners at the Court, are as ridiculous in the country, as the behaviour of the country is most mockable at the Court. You told me, you salute not at the Court, but you kiss
10 your hands; that courtesy would be uncleanly if courtiers were shepherds.

CLOWN: Instance, briefly: come, instance.

CORIN: Why we are still handling our ewes, and their fells you know are greasy.

15 CLOWN: Why do not your courtier's hands sweat? and is not the grease of a mutton, as wholesome as the sweat of a man? Shallow, shallow: a better instance I say: come.

CORIN: Besides, our hands are hard.

20 CLOWN: Your lips will feel them the sooner. Shallow again: a more sounder instance, come.

CORIN: And they are often tarr'd over, with the surgery of our sheep: and would you have us kiss tar? The courtier's hands are perfum'd with civet.

25 CLOWN: Most shallow man: thou worm's-meat in respect of a good piece of flesh indeed: learn of the wise and perpend: civet is of a baser birth than tar, the very uncleanly flux of a cat. Mend the instance shepherd.

CORIN: You have too courtly a wit, for me, I'll rest.

30 CLOWN: Will thou rest damn'd? God help thee shallow man: God make incision in thee, thou art raw.

CORIN: Sir, I am a true labourer, I earn that I eat: get that I wear: owe no man hate, envy no man's happiness: glad of other men's good: content with my harm; and the greatest of my pride, is to see my ewes graze, and my lambs suck.

CLOWN: That is another simple sin in you, to bring the ewes and the rams together, and to offer to get your liv- 5 ing, by the copulation of cattle, to be bawd to a bell-wether, and to betray a she-lamb of a twelve-month to a crooked-pated old cuckoldly ram, out of all reasonable match. If thou beest not damn'd for this, the devil him-self will have no shepherds, I cannot see else how thou 10 shouldst 'scape.

CORIN: Here comes young Master Ganymede, my new mistress's brother.

*Enter Rosalind.*

ROSALIND: *From the east to western Ind,* 15
  *No jewel is like Rosalind,*
  *Her worth being mounted on the wind,*
   *Through all the world bears Rosalind.*
  *All the pictures fairest lin'd,*
   *Are but black to Rosalind:* 20
  *Let no face be kept in mind,*
   *But the fair of Rosalind.*

CLOWN: I'll rhyme you so, eight years together; dinners, and suppers, and sleeping-hours excepted: it is the right butter-women's rank to market. 25

ROSALIND: Out fool.

CLOWN: For a taste.
  *If a hart do lack a hind,*
   *Let him seek out Rosalind:*
  *If the cat will after kind,* 30
   *So be sure will Rosalind:*
  *Winter garments must be lin'd,*
   *So must slender Rosalind:*

> They that reap must sheaf and bind,
> > Then to cart with Rosalind.
> Sweetest nut, hath sourest rind,
> > Such a nut is Rosalind.
5   > He that sweetest rose will find,
> > Must find love's prick, and Rosalind.

This is the very false gallop of verses, why do you infect yourself with them?

ROSALIND: Peace you dull fool, I found them on a tree.

10   CLOWN: Truly the tree yields bad fruit.

ROSALIND: I'll graff it with you, and then I shall graff it with a medlar: then it will be the earliest fruit i'th' country: for you'll be rotten ere you be half ripe, and that's the right virtue of the medlar.

15   CLOWN: You have said: but whether wisely or no, let the Forest judge.

*Enter Celia with a writing.*

ROSALIND: Peace, here comes my sister reading, stand aside.

20   CELIA: *Why should this a desert be,*
> *For it is unpeopled? No:*
> *Tongues I'll hang on every tree,*
> *That shall civil sayings show.*
> *Some, how brief the life of man*
25   > *Runs his erring pilgrimage,*
> *That the stretching of a span,*
> *Buckles in his sum of age;*
> *Some of violated vows,*
> *'Twixt the souls of friend, and friend:*
30   > *But upon the fairest boughs,*
> *Or at every sentence end;*
> *Will I Rosalind write,*
> *Teaching all that read, to know*

*The quintessence of every sprite,*
  *Heaven would in little show.*
*Therefore Heaven Nature charg'd,*
  *That one body should be fill'd*
*With all graces wide enlarg'd,*                    5
  *Nature presently distill'd*
*Helen's cheek, but not her heart,*
  *Cleopatra's majesty:*
*Atalanta's better part;*
  *Sad Lucretia's modesty.*                          10
*Thus Rosalind of many parts,*
  *By heavenly synod was devis'd,*
*Of many faces, eyes, and hearts,*
  *To have the touches dearest priz'd.*
*Heaven would that she these gifts should have,*    15
  *And I to live and die her slave.*

ROSALIND: O most gentle Jupiter, what tedious homily of love have you wearied your parishioners withal, and never cri'd, Have patience good people.

CELIA: How now, back friends: Shepherd, go off a little:  20
go with him sirrah.

CLOWN: Come shepherd, let us make an honourable retreat, though not with bag and baggage, yet with scrip and scrippage.

                    *Exeunt Corin and Clown.*        25

CELIA: Didst thou hear these verses?

ROSALIND: O yes, I heard them all, and more too, for some of them had in them more feet than the verses would bear.

CELIA: That's no matter: the feet might bear the verses.  30

ROSALIND: Ay, but the feet were lame, and could not bear themselves without the verse, and therefore stood lamely in the verse.

CELIA: But didst thou hear without wondering, how thy name should be hang'd and carved upon these trees?

ROSALIND: I was seven of the nine days out of the wonder, before you came: for look here what I found on a palm tree: I was never so be-rhym'd since Pythagoras' time that I was an Irish rat, which I can hardly remember.

CELIA: Trow you, who hath done this?

ROSALIND: Is it a man?

CELIA: And a chain that you once wore about his neck: change you colour?

ROSALIND: I prithee who?

CELIA: O Lord, Lord, it is a hard matter for friends to meet: but mountains may be remov'd with earthquakes, and so encounter.

ROSALIND: Nay, but who is it?

CELIA: Is it possible?

ROSALIND: Nay, I prithee now, with most petitionary vehemence, tell me who it is.

CELIA: O wonderful, wonderful, and most wonderful wonderful, and yet again wonderful, and after that out of all hooping.

ROSALIND: Good my complexion, dost thou think though I am caparison'd like a man, I have a doublet and hose in my disposition? One inch of delay more, is a South-sea of discovery. I prithee tell me, who is it quickly, and speak apace: I would thou couldst stammer, that thou might'st pour this conceal'd man out of thy mouth, as wine comes out of a narrow-mouth'd bottle; either too much at once, or none at all. I prithee take the cork out of thy mouth, that I may drink thy tidings.

CELIA: So you may put a man in your belly.

ROSALIND: Is he of God's making? What manner of man? Is his head worth a hat? Or his chin worth a beard?

CELIA: Nay, he hath but a little beard.

ROSALIND: Why God will send more, if the man will be thankful: let me stay the growth of his beard, if thou delay me not the knowledge of his chin.

CELIA: It is young Orlando, that tripp'd up the wrestler's heels, and your heart, both in an instant.

ROSALIND: Nay, but the devil take mocking: speak sad brow, and true maid.

CELIA: I' faith, coz, 'tis he.

ROSALIND: Orlando?

CELIA: Orlando.

ROSALIND: Alas the day, what shall I do with my doublet and hose? What did he when thou saw'st him? What said he? How look'd he? Wherein went he? What makes he here? Did he ask for me? Where remains he? How parted he with thee? And when shalt thou see him again? Answer me in one word.

CELIA: You must borrow me Gargantua's mouth first: 'tis a word too great for any mouth of this age's size, to say ay and no, to these particulars, is more than to answer in a catechism.

ROSALIND: But doth he know that I am in this Forest, and in man's apparel? Looks he as freshly, as he did the day he wrestled?

CELIA: It is as easy to count atomies as to resolve the propositions of a lover: but take a taste of my finding him, and relish it with good observance. I found him under a tree like a dropp'd acorn.

ROSALIND: It may well be call'd Jove's tree, when it drops forth fruit.

CELIA: Give me audience, good Madam.

ROSALIND: Proceed.

CELIA: There lay he stretch'd along like a wounded knight.

ROSALIND: Though it be pity to see such a sight, it well becomes the ground.

CELIA: Cry holla, to thy tongue, I prithee: it curvets unseasonably. He was furnish'd like a hunter.

5 ROSALIND: O ominous, he comes to kill my heart.

CELIA: I would sing my song without a burthen, thou bring'st me out of tune.

ROSALIND: Do you not know I am a woman, when I think, I must speak: sweet, say on.

10 *Enter Orlando and Jaques.*

CELIA: You bring me out. Soft, comes he not here?

ROSALIND: 'Tis he, slink by, and note him.

JAQUES: I thank you for your company, but good faith I had as lief have been myself alone.

15 ORLANDO: And so had I: but yet for fashion sake I thank you too, for your society.

JAQUES: God buy you, let's meet as little as we can.

ORLANDO: I do desire we may be better strangers.

JAQUES: I pray you mar no more trees with writing love-
20 songs in their barks.

ORLANDO: I pray you mar no more of my verses with reading them ill-favouredly.

JAQUES: Rosalind is your love's name?

ORLANDO: Yes, just.

25 JAQUES: I do not like her name.

ORLANDO: There was no thought of pleasing you when she was christen'd.

JAQUES: What stature is she of?

ORLANDO: Just as high as my heart.

30 JAQUES: You are full of pretty answers: have you not been acquainted with goldsmiths' wives, and conn'd them out of rings?

ORLANDO: Not so: but I answer you right painted cloth,

from whence you have studied your questions.

JAQUES: You have a nimble wit; I think 'twas made of Atalanta's heels. Will you sit down with me, and we two, will rail against our mistress the world, and all our misery.

ORLANDO: I will chide no breather in the world but my-  5
self against whom I know most faults.

JAQUES: The worst fault you have, is to be in love.

ORLANDO: 'Tis a fault I will not change, for your best virtues: I am weary of you.

JAQUES: By my troth, I was seeking for a fool, when I  10
found you.

ORLANDO: He is drown'd in the brook, look but in, and you shall see him.

JAQUES: There I shall see mine own figure.

ORLANDO: Which I take to be either a fool, or a cipher.  15

JAQUES: I'll tarry no longer with you, farewell good Signior Love.

ORLANDO: I am glad of your departure: adieu good Monsieur Melancholy.

*Exit Jaques.*  20

ROSALIND: I will speak to him like a saucy lackey, and under that habit play the knave with him; do you hear forester?

ORLANDO: Very well, what would you?

ROSALIND: I pray you, what is't o'clock?  25

ORLANDO: You should ask me what time o' day: there's no clock in the Forest.

ROSALIND: Then there is no true lover in the Forest, else sighing every minute, and groaning every hour would detect the lazy foot of Time, as well as a clock.  30

ORLANDO: And why not the swift foot of Time? had not that been as proper?

ROSALIND: By no means sir: Time travels in divers paces,

with divers persons: I'll tell you who Time ambles
withal, who Time trots withal, who Time gallops withal,
and who he stands still withal.

ORLANDO: I prithee, who doth he trot withal?

5 ROSALIND: Marry he trots hard with a young maid, between the contract of her marriage, and the day it is
solemniz'd: if the interim be but a se'nnight, Time's pace
is so hard, that it seems the length of seven year.

ORLANDO: Who ambles Time withal?

10 ROSALIND: With a priest that lacks Latin, and a rich man
that hath not the gout; for the one sleeps easily because
he cannot study, and the other lives merrily, because he
feels no pain: the one lacking the burthen of lean and
wasteful learning; the other knowing no burthen of

15 heavy tedious penury. These Time ambles withal.

ORLANDO: Who doth he gallop withal?

ROSALIND: With a thief to the gallows: for though he go
as softly as foot can fall, he thinks himself too soon there.

ORLANDO: Who stays it still withal?

20 ROSALIND: With lawyers in the vacation: for they sleep
between term and term, and then they perceive not how
Time moves.

ORLANDO: Where dwell you pretty youth?

ROSALIND: With this shepherdess my sister: here in the
25 skirts of the Forest, like fringe upon a petticoat.

ORLANDO: Are you native of this place?

ROSALIND: As the cony that you see dwell where she is
kindled.

ORLANDO: Your accent is something finer, than you could
30 purchase in so removed a dwelling.

ROSALIND: I have been told so of many: but indeed, an
old religious uncle of mine taught me to speak, who was
in his youth an inland man, one that knew courtship too

well: for there he fell in love. I have heard him read
many lectures against it, and I thank God, I am not a
woman to be touch'd with so many giddy offences as he
hath generally tax'd their whole sex withal.

ORLANDO: Can you remember any of the principal evils, 5
that he laid to the charge of women?

ROSALIND: There were none principal, they were all like
one another, as half-pence are, every one fault seeming
monstrous, till his fellow-fault came to match it.

ORLANDO: I prithee recount some of them. 10

ROSALIND: No: I will not cast away my physic, but on
those that are sick. There is a man haunts the Forest,
that abuses our young plants with carving *Rosalind* on
their barks; hangs odes upon hawthorns, and elegies on
brambles: all (forsooth) deifying the name of Rosalind. 15
If I could meet that fancy-monger, I would give him
some good counsel for he seems to have the quotidian
of love upon him.

ORLANDO: I am he that is so love-shak'd, I pray you tell
me your remedy. 20

ROSALIND: There is none of my uncle's marks upon you:
he taught me how to know a man in love: in which cage
of rushes, I am sure you are not prisoner.

ORLANDO: What were his marks?

ROSALIND: A lean cheek, which you have not: a blue eye 25
and sunken, which you have not: an unquestionable
spirit, which you have not: a beard neglected, which you
have not: (but I pardon you for that, for simply your
having in beard, is a younger brother's revenue) then
your hose should be ungarter'd, your bonnet unbanded, 30
your sleeve unbutton'd, your shoe unti'd, and every thing
about you, demonstrating a careless desolation: but you
are no such man: you are rather point-device in your

accoutrements, as loving yourself, than seeming the lover of any other.

ORLANDO: Fair youth, I would I could make thee believe I love.

5 ROSALIND: Me believe it? You may as soon make her that you love believe it, which I warrant she is apter to do, than to confess she does: that is one of the points, in the which women still give the lie to their consciences. But in good sooth, are you he that hangs the verses on

10 the trees, wherein Rosalind is so admired?

ORLANDO: I swear to thee youth, by the white hand of Rosalind, I am that he, that unfortunate he.

ROSALIND: But are you so much in love, as your rhymes speak?

15 ORLANDO: Neither rhyme nor reason can express how much.

ROSALIND: Love is merely a madness, and I tell you, deserves as well a dark house, and a whip, as madmen do: and the reason why they are not so punish'd and cured,

20 is that the lunacy is so ordinary, that the whippers are in love too: yet I profess curing it by counsel.

ORLANDO: Did you ever cure any so?

ROSALIND: Yes one, and in this manner. He was to imagine me his love, his mistress; and I set him every day to

25 woo me: at which time would I, being but a moonish youth, grieve, be effeminate, changeable, longing, and liking, proud, fantastical, apish, shallow, inconstant, full of tears, full of smiles; for every passion something, and for no passion truly any thing; as boys and women are

30 for the most part, cattle of this colour: would now like him, now loathe him: then entertain him, then forswear him: now weep for him, then spit at him; that I drave my suitor from his mad humour of love, to a living

humour of madness, which was to forswear the full stream
of the world, and to live in a nook merely monastic:
and thus I cur'd him, and this way will I take upon me
to wash your liver as clean as a sound sheep's heart, that
there shall not be one spot of love in't.                                5

ORLANDO: I would not be cured, youth.

ROSALIND: I would cure you, if you would but call me
Rosalind, and come every day to my cote, and woo me.

ORLANDO: Now by the faith of my love, I will; tell me
where it is.                                                                        10

ROSALIND: Go with me to it, and I'll show it you: and by
the way, you shall tell me, where in the forest you live:
will you go?

ORLANDO: With all my heart, good youth.

ROSALIND: Nay, you must call me Rosalind: come sister,     15
will you go?              *Exeunt.*

# III. 3

*Enter Clown, Audrey and Jaques.*

CLOWN: Come apace good Audrey, I will fetch up your     20
goats, Audrey: and how Audrey, am I the man yet?
doth my simple feature content you?

AUDREY: Your features, Lord warrant us: what features?

CLOWN: I am here with thee, and thy goats, as the most
capricious poet honest Ovid was among the Goths.               25

JAQUES: O knowledge ill-inhabited, worse than Jove in a
thatch'd house.

CLOWN: When a man's verses cannot be understood, nor
a man's good wit seconded with the forward child understanding, it strikes a man more dead than a great reckon-    30
ing in a little room: truly, I would the gods had made
thee poetical.

AUDREY: I do not know what poetical is: is it honest in deed and word: is it a true thing?

CLOWN: No truly: for the truest poetry is the most feigning, and lovers are given to poetry: and what they swear
5　in poetry, may be said as lovers, they do feign.

AUDREY: Do you wish then that the gods had made me poetical?

CLOWN: I do truly: for thou swear'st to me thou art honest; now if thou wert a poet, I might have some hope
10　thou didst feign.

AUDREY: Would you not have me honest?

CLOWN: No truly, unless thou wert hard-favour'd: for honesty coupled to beauty, is to have honey a sauce to sugar.

JAQUES: A material fool.

15　AUDREY: Well, I am not fair, and therefore I pray the gods make me honest.

CLOWN: Truly, and to cast away honesty upon a foul slut, were to put good meat into an unclean dish.

AUDREY: I am not a slut, though I thank the gods I am foul.

20　CLOWN: Well, praised be the gods, for thy foulness; sluttishness may come hereafter. But be it, as it may be, I will marry thee: and to that end, I have been with Sir Oliver Mar-text, the vicar of the next village, who hath promis'd to meet me in this place of the Forest, and to
25　couple us.

JAQUES: I would fain see this meeting.

AUDREY: Well, the gods give us joy.

CLOWN: Amen. A man may if he were of a fearful heart, stagger in this attempt: for here we have no temple but
30　the wood, no assembly but horn-beasts. But what though? Courage. As horns are odious, they are necessary. It is said, many a man knows no end of his goods; right: many a man has good horns, and knows no end of

them. Well, that is the dowry of his wife, 'tis none of his own getting; horns, even so poor men alone: no, no, the noblest deer hath them as huge as the rascal: is the single man therefore blessed? No, as a wall'd town is more worthier than a village, so is the forehead of a married 5 man, more honourable than the bare brow of a bachelor: and by how much defence is better than no skill, by so much is a horn more precious than to want.

*Enter Sir Oliver Mar-text.*

Here comes Sir Oliver: Sir Oliver Mar-text you are well 10 met. Will you dispatch us here under this tree, or shall we go with you to your chapel?

SIR OLIVER: Is there none here to give the woman?

CLOWN: I will not take her on gift of any man.

SIR OLIVER: Truly she must be given, or the marriage is 15 not lawful.

JAQUES: Proceed, proceed: I'll give her.

CLOWN: Good even good Master What-ye-call't: how do you sir, you are very well met: God 'ild you for your last company, I am very glad to see you; even a toy in 20 hand here sir: nay, pray be cover'd.

JAQUES: Will you be married, motley?

CLOWN: As the ox hath his bow sir, the horse his curb, and the falcon her bells, so man hath his desires, and as pigeons bill, so wedlock would be nibbling. 25

JAQUES: And will you (being a man of your breeding) be married under a bush like a beggar? Get you to church, and have a good priest that can tell you what marriage is, this fellow will but join you together, as they join wainscot, then one of you will prove a shrunk panel, 30 and like green timber, warp, warp.

CLOWN: I am not in the mind, but I were better to be married of him than of another, for he is not like to

marry me well: and not being well married, it will be
a good excuse for me hereafter, to leave my wife.

JAQUES: Go thou with me, and let me counsel thee.

CLOWN: Come sweet Audrey,

5 We must be married, or we must live in bawdry:
Farewell good Master Oliver: not O sweet Oliver, O
brave Oliver leave me not behind thee: but wind away,
begone I say, I will not to wedding with thee.

SIR OLIVER: 'Tis no matter; ne'er a fantastical knave of
10 them all shall flout me out of my calling.

*Exeunt.*

# III. 4

*Enter Rosalind and Celia.*

ROSALIND: Never talk to me, I will weep.

15 CELIA: Do I prithee, but yet have the grace to consider,
that tears do not become a man.

ROSALIND: But have I not cause to weep?

CELIA: As good cause as one would desire, therefore weep.

ROSALIND: His very hair is of the dissembling colour.

20 CELIA: Something browner than Judas's: marry his kisses
are Judas's own children.

ROSALIND: I' faith his hair is of a good colour.

CELIA: An excellent colour: your chestnut was ever the
only colour.

25 ROSALIND: And his kissing is as full of sanctity, as the
touch of holy bread.

CELIA: He hath bought a pair of cast lips of Diana: a nun
of winter's sisterhood kisses not more religiously, the
very ice of chastity is in them.

30 ROSALIND: But why did he swear he would come this
morning, and comes not?

CELIA: Nay certainly there is no truth in him.

ROSALIND: Do you think so?

CELIA: Yes, I think he is not a pick-purse, nor a horse-stealer, but for his verity in love, I do think him as concave as a covered goblet, or a worm-eaten nut. 5

ROSALIND: Not true in love?

CELIA: Yes, when he is in, but I think he is not in.

ROSALIND: You have heard him swear downright he was.

CELIA: Was, is not is: besides, the oath of a lover is no stronger than the word of a tapster, they are both the 10 confirmer of false reckonings; he attends here in the Forest on the Duke your father.

ROSALIND: I met the Duke yesterday, and had much question with him: he ask'd me of what parentage I was; I told him, of as good as he, so he laugh'd and let me go. 15 But what talk we of fathers, when there is such a man as Orlando?

CELIA: O that's a brave man, he writes brave verses, speaks brave words, swears brave oaths, and breaks them bravely, quite traverse athwart the heart of his lover, as 20 a puisny tilter, that spurs his horse but on one side, breaks his staff like a noble goose; but all's brave that youth mounts, and folly guides: who comes here?

*Enter Corin.*

CORIN: Mistress and master, you have oft enquired 25
    After the shepherd that complain'd of love,
    Who you saw sitting by me on the turf,
    Praising the proud disdainful shepherdess
    That was his mistress.

CELIA: Well: and what of him? 30

CORIN: If you will see a pageant truly play'd
    Between the pale complexion of true love,
    And the red glow of scorn and proud disdain,

Go hence a little, and I shall conduct you
If you will mark it.

ROSALIND: O come, let us remove,
The sight of lovers feedeth those in love:
5   Bring us to this sight, and you shall say
I'll prove a busy actor in their play.

*Exeunt.*

# III. 5

*Enter Silvius and Phebe*

10 SILVIUS: Sweet Phebe do not scorn me, do not Phebe
Say that you love me not, but say not so
In bitterness; the common executioner
Whose heart th' accustom'd sight of death makes hard
Falls not the axe upon the humbled neck,
15   But first begs pardon: will you sterner be
Than he that dies and lives by bloody drops?

*Enter Rosalind, Celia and Corin.*

PHEBE: I would not be thy executioner,
I fly thee, for I would not injure thee:
20   Thou tell'st me there is murder in mine eye,
'Tis pretty sure, and very probable,
That eyes that are the frail'st, and softest things,
Who shut their coward gates on atomies,
Should be call'd tyrants, butchers, murtherers.
25   Now I do frown on thee with all my heart,
And if mine eyes can wound, now let them kill thee:
Now counterfeit to swoon, why now fall down,
Or if thou canst not, oh for shame, for shame,
Lie not, to say mine eyes are murtherers:
30   Now show the wound mine eye hath made in thee,
Scratch thee but with a pin, and there remains

Some scar of it: lean but upon a rush
The cicatrice and capable impressure
Thy palm some moment keeps: but now mine eyes
Which I have darted at thee, hurt thee not,
Nor am I sure there is no force in eyes                    5
That can do hurt.
SILVIUS: O dear Phebe,
  If ever (as that ever may be near)
  You meet in some fresh cheek the power of fancy,
  Then shall you know the wounds invisible              10
  That Love's keen arrows make.
PHEBE: But till that time
  Come not thou near me: and when that time comes,
  Afflict me with thy mocks, pity me not,
  As till that time I shall not pity thee.                15
ROSALIND: And why I pray you? Who might be your
    mother
  That you insult, exult, and all at once
  Over the wretched? What though you have no beauty,
  As by my faith, I see no more in you                   20
  Than without candle may go dark to bed:
  Must you be therefore proud and pitiless?
  Why what means this? Why do you look on me?
  I see no more in you than in the ordinary
  Of Nature's sale-work. 'Od's my little life,          25
  I think she means to tangle my eyes too:
  No faith proud mistress, hope not after it,
  'Tis not your inky brows, your black silk hair,
  Your bugle eyeballs, nor your cheek of cream
  That can entame my spirits to your worship:           30
  You foolish shepherd, wherefore do you follow her
  Like foggy South puffing with wind and rain,
  You are a thousand times a properer man

Than she a woman. 'Tis such fools as you
That makes the world full of ill-favour'd children:
'Tis not her glass, but you that flatters her,
And out of you she sees herself more proper
5  Than any of her lineaments can show her:
But mistress, know yourself, down on your knees
And thank heaven, fasting, for a good man's love;
For I must tell you friendly in your ear,
Sell when you can, you are not for all markets:
10  Cry the man mercy, love him, take his offer,
Foul is most foul, being foul to be a scoffer,
So take her to thee shepherd, fare you well.

PHEBE: Sweet youth, I pray you chide a year together, I
had rather hear you chide, than this man woo.

15  ROSALIND: He's fallen in love with your foulness, and
she'll fall in love with my anger. If it be so, as fast as she
answers thee with frowning looks, I'll sauce her with
bitter words: why look you so upon me?

PHEBE: For no ill will I bear you.

20  ROSALIND: I pray you do not fall in love with me,
For I am falser than vows made in wine:
Besides, I like you not: if you will know my house,
'Tis at the tuft of olives, here hard by:
Will you go sister? Shepherd ply her hard:
25  Come sister: Shepherdess, look on him better
And be not proud, though all the world could see,
None could be so abus'd in sight as he.
Come, to our flock.

*Exeunt Rosalind, Celia and Corin.*

30  PHEBE: Dead shepherd, now I find thy saw of might,
Who ever lov'd, that lov'd not at first sight?

SILVIUS: Sweet Phebe.

PHEBE: Ha: what say'st thou Silvius?

SILVIUS: Sweet Phebe pity me.

PHEBE: Why I am sorry for thee gentle Silvius.

SILVIUS: Wherever sorrow is, relief would be:
  If you do sorrow at my grief in love,
  By giving love your sorrow, and my grief      5
  Were both extermin'd.

PHEBE: Thou hast my love, is not that neighbourly?

SILVIUS: I would have you.

PHEBE: Why that were covetousness:
  Silvius; the time was, that I hated thee;      10
  And yet it is not, that I bear thee love,
  But since that thou canst talk of love so well,
  Thy company, which erst was irksome to me
  I will endure; and I'll employ thee too:
  But do not look for further recompense      15
  Than thine own gladness, that thou art employ'd.

SILVIUS: So holy, and so perfect is my love,
  And I in such a poverty of grace,
  That I shall think it a most plenteous crop
  To glean the broken ears after the man      20
  That the main harvest reaps: loose now and then
  A scatter'd smile, and that I'll live upon.

PHEBE: Know'st thou the youth that spoke to me erewhile?

SILVIUS: Not very well, but I have met him oft,
  And he hath bought the cottage and the bounds      25
  That the old carlot once was master of.

PHEBE: Think not I love him, though I ask for him,
  'Tis but a peevish boy, yet he talks well,
  But what care I for words? yet words do well
  When he that speaks them pleases those that hear:      30
  It is a pretty youth, not very pretty,
  But sure he's proud, and yet his pride becomes him;
  He'll make a proper man: the best thing in him

Is his complexion: and faster than his tongue
Did make offence, his eye did heal it up:
He is not very tall, yet for his years he's tall:
His leg is but so so, and yet 'tis well:
5   There was a pretty redness in his lip,
A little riper, and more lusty red
Than that mix'd in his cheek: 'twas just the difference
Betwixt the constant red, and mingled damask.
There be some women Silvius, had they mark'd him
10  In parcels as I did, would have gone near
To fall in love with him: but for my part
I love him not, nor hate him not: and yet
I have more cause to hate him than to love him,
For what had he to do to chide at me?
15  He said mine eyes were black, and my hair black,
And now I am remember'd, scorn'd at me:
I marvel why I answer'd not again,
But that's all one: omittance is no quittance:
I'll write to him a very taunting letter,
20  And thou shalt bear it, wilt thou Silvius?
SILVIUS: Phebe, with all my heart.
PHEBE: I'll write it straight:
The matter's in my head, and in my heart,
I will be bitter with him, and passing short;
25  Go with me Silvius.

*Exeunt.*

# IV. 1

*Enter Rosalind, and Celia, and Jaques.*

JAQUES: I prithee, pretty youth, let me be better acquain-
30  ted with thee.

ROSALIND: They say you are a melancholy fellow.

JAQUES: I am so: I do love it better than laughing.

ROSALIND: Those that are in extremity of either, are abo-
minable fellows, and betray themselves to every modern
censure, worse than drunkards.

JAQUES: Why, 'tis good to be sad and say nothing. 5

ROSALIND: Why then 'tis good to be a post.

JAQUES: I have neither the scholar's melancholy, which is
emulation: nor the musician's, which is fantastical; nor
the courtier's, which is proud: nor the soldier's, which
is ambitious: nor the lawyer's, which is politic: nor 10
the lady's, which is nice: nor the lover's, which is all
these: but it is a melancholy of mine own compounded
of many simples, extracted from many objects, and indeed
the sundry contemplation of my travels, in which by often
rumination, wraps me in a most humorous sadness. 15

ROSALIND: A traveller: by my faith you have great reason
to be sad: I fear you have sold your own lands, to see
other men's; then to have seen much, and to have nothing, is to have rich eyes and poor hands.

JAQUES: Yes, I have gain'd my experience. 20

*Enter Orlando.*

ROSALIND: And your experience makes you sad: I had
rather have a fool to make me merry, than experience
to make me sad, and to travel for it too.

ORLANDO: Good-day, and happiness, dear Rosalind. 25

JAQUES: Nay then God buy you, and you talk in blank verse.

*Exit.*

ROSALIND: Farewell Monsieur Traveller: look you lisp,
and wear strange suits; disable all the benefits of your
own country: be out of love with your nativity, and 30
almost chide God for making you that countenance you
are; or I will scarce think you have swam in a gondola.
Why how now Orlando, where have you been all this

while? You a lover? And you serve me such another
trick, never come in my sight more.

ORLANDO: My fair Rosalind, I come within an hour of
my promise.

5 ROSALIND: Break an hour's promise in love? He that will
divide a minute into a thousand parts, and break but a
part of the thousandth part of a minute in the affairs of
love, it may be said of him that Cupid hath clapp'd him
o' th' shoulder, but I'll warrant him heart-whole.

10 ORLANDO: Pardon me dear Rosalind.

ROSALIND: Nay, and you be so tardy, come no more in
my sight, I had as lief be woo'd of a snail.

ORLANDO: Of a snail?

ROSALIND: Ay, of a snail: for though he comes slowly,
15 he carries his house on his head; a better jointure I think
than you make a woman: besides, he brings his destiny
with him.

ORLANDO: What's that?

ROSALIND: Why horns: which such as you are fain to be
20 beholding to your wives for: but he comes armed in his
fortune, and prevents the slander of his wife.

ORLANDO: Virtue is no horn-maker: and my Rosalind is
virtuous.

ROSALIND: And I am your Rosalind.

25 CELIA: It pleases him to call you so: but he hath a Rosalind
of a better leer than you.

ROSALIND: Come, woo me, woo me: for now I am in a
holiday humour, and like enough to consent: what would
you say to me now, and I were your very, very Rosalind?

30 ORLANDO: I would kiss before I spoke.

ROSALIND: Nay, you were better speak first, and when
you were gravell'd, for lack of matter, you might take
occasion to kiss: very good orators when they are out,

they will spit, and for lovers, lacking (God warn us) matter, the cleanliest shift is to kiss.

ORLANDO: How if the kiss be denied?

ROSALIND: Then she puts you to entreaty, and there begins new matter. 5

ORLANDO: Who could be out, being before his beloved mistress?

ROSALIND: Marry that should you if I were your mistress, or I should think my honesty ranker than my wit.

ORLANDO: What, of my suit? 10

ROSALIND: Not out of your apparel, and yet out of your suit: am not I your Rosalind?

ORLANDO: I take some joy to say you are, because I would be talking of her.

ROSALIND: Well, in her person, I say I will not have you. 15

ORLANDO: Then in mine own person, I die.

ROSALIND: No faith, die by attorney: the poor world is almost six thousand years old, and in all this time there was not any man died in his own person (*videlicet*) in a love-cause: Troilus had his brains dash'd out with a 20 Grecian club, yet he did what he could to die before, and he is one of the patterns of love. Leander, he would have liv'd many a fair year though Hero had turn'd nun; if it had not been for a hot midsummer night, for (good youth) he went but forth to wash him in the 25 Hellespont, and being taken with the cramp, was drown'd, and the foolish chroniclers of that age, found it was Hero of Sestos. But these are all lies, men have died from time to time, and worms have eaten them, but not for love. 30

ORLANDO: I would not have my right Rosalind of this mind, for I protest her frown might kill me.

ROSALIND: By this hand, it will not kill a fly: but come,

now I will be your Rosalind in a more coming-on disposition: and ask me what you will, I will grant it.

ORLANDO: Then love me Rosalind.

ROSALIND: Yes faith will I, Fridays and Saturdays, and all.

5 ORLANDO: And wilt thou have me?

ROSALIND: Ay, and twenty such.

ORLANDO: What sayest thou?

ROSALIND: Are you not good?

ORLANDO: I hope so.

10 ROSALIND: Why then, can one desire too much of a good thing: come sister, you shall be the priest, and marry us: give me your hand Orlando: what do you say sister?

ORLANDO: Pray thee marry us.

CELIA: I cannot say the words.

15 ROSALIND: You must begin, Will you Orlando.

CELIA: Go to: Will you Orlando, have to wife this Rosalind?

ORLANDO: I will.

ROSALIND: Ay, but when?

ORLANDO: Why now, as fast as she can marry us.

20 ROSALIND: Then you must say, I take thee Rosalind for wife.

ORLANDO: I take thee Rosalind for wife.

ROSALIND: I might ask you for your commission, but I do take thee Orlando for my husband: there's a girl goes before the priest, and certainly a woman's thought runs

25 before her actions.

ORLANDO: So do all thoughts, they are wing'd.

ROSALIND: Now tell me how long you would have her, after you have possess'd her?

ORLANDO: For ever, and a day.

30 ROSALIND: Say a day, without the ever: no, no Orlando, men are April when they woo, December when they wed: maids are May when they are maids, but the sky changes when they are wives: I will be more jealous of

thee, than a Barbary cock-pigeon over his hen, more
clamorous than a parrot against rain, more new-fangled
than an ape, more giddy in my desires, than a monkey:
I will weep for nothing, like Diana in the fountain, and
I will do that when you are dispos'd to be merry: I will 5
laugh like a hyen, and that when thou art inclin'd to sleep.

ORLANDO: But will my Rosalind do so?

ROSALIND: By my life, she will do as I do.

ORLANDO: O but she is wise.

ROSALIND: Or else she could not have the wit to do this: 10
the wiser, the waywarder: make the doors upon a woman's wit, and it will out at the casement: shut that, and
'twill out at the key-hole: stop that, 'twill fly with the
smoke out at the chimney.

ORLANDO: A man that had a wife with such a wit, he 15
might say, Wit whither wilt?

ROSALIND: Nay, you might keep that check for it, till you
met your wife's wit going to your neighbour's bed.

ORLANDO: And what wit could wit have, to excuse that?

ROSALIND: Marry to say, she came to seek you there: you 20
shall never take her without her answer, unless you take
her without her tongue: oh that woman that cannot
make her fault her husband's occasion, let her never
nurse her child herself, for she will breed it like a fool.

ORLANDO: For these two hours Rosalind, I will leave thee. 25

ROSALIND: Alas, dear love, I cannot lack thee two hours.

ORLANDO: I must attend the Duke at dinner, by two o'
clock I will be with thee again.

ROSALIND: Ay, go your ways, go your ways: I knew what
you would prove, my friends told me as much, and I 30
thought no less: that flattering tongue of yours won me:
'tis but one cast away, and so come death: two o'clock
is your hour?

ORLANDO: Ay, sweet Rosalind.

ROSALIND: By my troth, and in good earnest, and so God
mend me, and by all pretty oaths that are not dangerous,
if you break one jot of your promise, or come one min-
5  ute behind your hour, I will think you the most pathe-
tical break-promise, and the most hollow lover, and the
most unworthy of her you call Rosalind, that may be
chosen out of the gross band of the unfaithful: therefore
beware my censure, and keep your promise.

10 ORLANDO: With no less religion, than if thou wert indeed
my Rosalind: so adieu.

ROSALIND: Well, Time is the old justice that examines all
such offenders, and let Time try: adieu.

*Exit Orlando.*

15 CELIA: You have simply misus'd our sex in your love-
prate: we must have your doublet and hose pluck'd over
your head, and show the world what the bird hath done
to her own nest.

ROSALIND: O coz, coz, coz: my pretty little coz, that thou
20  didst know how many fathom deep I am in love: but it
cannot be sounded: my affection hath an unknown bottom, like the Bay of Portugal.

CELIA: Or rather bottomless, that as fast as you pour
affection in it, it runs out.

25 ROSALIND: No, that same wicked bastard of Venus, that
was begot of thought, conceiv'd of spleen, and born of
madness, that blind rascally boy, that abuses every one's
eyes, because his own are out, let him be judge, how
deep I am in love: I'll tell thee Aliena, I cannot be out
30  of the sight of Orlando: I'll go find a shadow, and sigh
till he come.

CELIA: And I'll sleep.

*Exeunt.*

## IV.2

*Enter Jaques and Lords, Foresters.*

JAQUES: Which is he that killed the deer?

A LORD: Sir, it was I.

JAQUES: Let's present him to the Duke like a Roman con-    5
queror, and it would do well to set the deer's horns upon
his head, for a branch of victory; have you no song
forester for this purpose?

FORESTER: Yes sir.

JAQUES: Sing it: 'tis no matter how it be in tune, so it    10
make noise enough.

MUSIC, SONG.

FORESTER: *What shall he have that kill'd the deer?*
*His leather skins, and horns to wear:*
*Then sing him home, the rest shall bear*    15
*This burthen.*
*Take thou no scorn to wear the horn,*
*It was a crest ere thou wast born,*
*Thy father's father wore it,*
*And thy father bore it,*    20
*The horn, the horn, the lusty horn,*
*Is not a thing to laugh to scorn.*
*Exeunt.*

## IV.3

*Enter Rosalind and Celia.*    25

ROSALIND: How say you now, is it not past two o'clock?
And here much Orlando.

CELIA: I warrant you, with pure love, and troubled brain,
he hath ta'en his bow and arrows, and is gone forth to
sleep: look who comes here.    30

*Enter Silvius.*

SILVIUS: My errand is to you, fair youth.
　　My gentle Phebe, bid me give you this:
　　I know not the contents, but as I guess
5　　By the stern brow, and waspish action
　　Which she did use, as she was writing of it,
　　It bears an angry tenure; pardon me,
　　I am but as a guiltless messenger.

ROSALIND: Patience herself would startle at this letter,
10　　And play the swaggerer, bear this, bear all:
　　She says I am not fair, that I lack manners,
　　She calls me proud, and that she could not love me
　　Were man as rare as phœnix: 'Od's my will,
　　Her love is not the hare that I do hunt,
15　　Why writes she so to me? Well, shepherd, well,
　　This is a letter of your own device.

SILVIUS: No, I protest, I know not the contents,
　　Phebe did write it.

ROSALIND: Come, come, you are a fool,
20　　And turn'd into the extremity of love.
　　I saw her hand, she has a leathern hand,
　　A freestone-coloured hand: I verily did think
　　That her old gloves were on, but 'twas her hands:
　　She has a huswife's hand, but that's no matter:
25　　I say she never did invent this letter,
　　This is a man's invention, and his hand.

SILVIUS: Sure it is hers.

ROSALIND: Why, tis a boisterous and a cruel style,
　　A style for challengers: why, she defies me,
30　　Like Turk to Christian: women's gentle brain
　　Could not drop forth such giant rude invention,
　　Such Ethiope words, blacker in their effect
　　Than in their countenance: will you hear the letter?

SILVIUS: So please you, for I never heard it yet:
  Yet heard too much of Phebe's cruelty.
ROSALIND: She Phebes me: mark how the tyrant writes.
  [Reads—] *Art thou god, to shepherd turn'd?*
  *That a maiden's heart hath burn'd.*     5
  *Can a woman rail thus?*
SILVIUS: Call you this railing?
ROSALIND: [Reads—]
  *Why, thy godhead laid apart,*
  *Warr'st thou with a woman's heart?*     10
  *Did you ever hear such railing?*
  *Whiles the eye of man did woo me,*
  *That could do no vengeance to me.*
  *Meaning me a beast.*
  *If the scorn of your bright eyne*     15
  *Have power to raise such love in mine,*
  *Alack, in me, what strange effect*
  *Would they work in mild aspect?*
  *Whiles you chid me, I did love,*
  *How then might your prayers move?*     20
  *He that brings this love to thee,*
  *Little knows this love in me:*
  *And by him seal up thy mind,*
  *Whether that thy youth and kind*
  *Will the faithful offer take*     25
  *Of me, and all that I can make,*
  *Or else by him my love deny,*
  *And then I'll study how to die.*
SILVIUS: Call you this chiding?
CELIA: Alas poor shepherd.     30
ROSALIND: Do you pity him? No, he deserves no pity: wilt
  thou love such a woman? What, to make thee an instru-
  ment, and play false strains upon thee? not to be endur'd.

Well, go your way to her (for I see love hath made thee
a tame snake); and say this to her; that if she love me, I
charge her to love thee: if she will not, I will never have
her, unless thou entreat for her: if you be a true lover
5      hence, and not a word: for here comes more company.

*Exit Silvius.*
*Enter Oliver.*

OLIVER: Good morrow, fair ones: pray you (if you know)
Where in the purlieus of this Forest, stands
10     A sheep-cote, fenc'd about with olive-trees?

CELIA: West of this place, down in the neighbour bottom
The rank of osiers, by the murmuring stream
Left on your right hand, brings you to the place:
But at this hour, the house doth keep itself,
15     There's none within.

OLIVER: If that an eye may profit by a tongue,
Then should I know you by description,
Such garments, and such years: The boy is fair,
Of female favour, and bestows himself
20     Like a ripe sister: the woman low
And browner than her brother: are not you
The owner of the house I did enquire for?

CELIA: It is no boast, being ask'd, to say we are.

OLIVER: Orlando doth commend him to you both,
25     And to that youth he calls his Rosalind,
He sends this bloody napkin; are you he?

ROSALIND: I am: what must we understand by this?

OLIVER: Some of my shame, if you will know of me
What man I am, and how, and why, and where
30     This handkercher was stain'd.

CELIA: I pray you tell it.

OLIVER: When last the young Orlando parted from you,
He left a promise to return again

Within an hour, and pacing through the forest,
Chewing the food of sweet and bitter fancy,
Lo what befel: he threw his eye aside,
And mark what object did present itself
Under an old oak, whose boughs were moss'd with age     5
And high top, bald with dry antiquity:
A wretched ragged man, o'er grown with hair
Lay sleeping on his back; about his neck
A green and gilded snake had wreath'd itself,
Who with her head, nimble in threats approach'd     10
The opening of his mouth: but suddenly
Seeing Orlando, it unlink'd itself,
And with indented glides, did slip away
Into a bush, under which bush's shade
A lioness, with udders all drawn dry,     15
Lay couching head on ground, with catlike watch,
When that the sleeping man should stir; for 'tis
The royal disposition of that beast
To prey on nothing, that doth seem as dead:
This seen, Orlando did approach the man,     20
And found it was his brother, his elder brother.

CELIA: O I have heard him speak of that same brother,
And he did render him the most unnatural
That liv'd amongst men.

OLIVER: And well he might so do,     25
For well I know he was unnatural.

ROSALIND: But to Orlando: did he leave him there
Food to the suck'd and hungry lioness?

OLIVER: Twice did he turn his back, and purpos'd so:
But kindness, nobler ever than revenge,     30
And Nature stronger than his just occasion,
Made him give battle to the lioness:
Who quickly fell before him, in which hurtling

From miserable slumber I awaked.

CELIA: Are you his brother?

ROSALIND: Was't you he rescu'd?

CELIA: Was't you that did so oft contrive to kill him?

5   OLIVER: 'Twas I: but 'tis not I: I do not shame
    To tell you what I was, since my conversion
    So sweetly tastes, being the thing I am.

ROSALIND: But for the bloody napkin?

OLIVER: By and by:

10  When from the first to last betwixt us two,
    Tears our recountments had most kindly bath'd,
    As how I came into that desert place.
    In brief, he led me to the gentle Duke,
    Who gave me fresh array, and entertainment,
15  Committing me unto my brother's love,
    Who led me instantly into his cave,
    There stripp'd himself, and here upon his arm
    The lioness had torn some flesh away,
    Which all this while had bled; and now he fainted,
20  And cried in fainting upon Rosalind.
    Brief, I recover'd him, bound up his wound,
    And after some small space, being strong at heart,
    He sent me hither, stranger as I am
    To tell this story, that you might excuse
25  His broken promise, and to give this napkin
    Dyed in his blood, unto the shepherd youth,
    That he in sport doth call his Rosalind.

CELIA: Why how now Ganymede, sweet Ganymede.

OLIVER: Many will swoon when they do look on blood.

30  CELIA: There is more in it; Cousin Ganymede.

OLIVER: Look, he recovers.

ROSALIND: I would I were at home.

CELIA: We'll lead you thither:

I pray you will you take him by the arm.

OLIVER: Be of good cheer, youth: you a man? you lack
a man's heart.

ROSALIND: I do so, I confess it: ah, sirrah, a body would
think this was well counterfeited, I pray you tell your     5
brother how well I counterfeited: heigh-ho.

OLIVER: This was not counterfeit, there is too great testi-
mony in your complexion, that it was a passion of earnest.

ROSALIND: Counterfeit, I assure you.

OLIVER: Well then, take a good heart, and counterfeit to     10
be a man.

ROSALIND: So I do: but i' faith, I should have been a
woman by right.

CELIA: Come, you look paler and paler: pray you draw
homewards: good sir, go with us.     15

OLIVER: That will I: for I must bear answer back
How you excuse my brother, Rosalind.

ROSALIND: I shall devise something: but I pray you commend my counterfeiting to him: will you go?

*Exeunt.*     20


# V. I

### *Enter Clown and Audrey.*

CLOWN: We shall find a time Audrey, patience gentle
Audrey.

AUDREY: Faith the Priest was good enough, for all the old     25
gentleman's saying.

CLOWN: A most wicked Sir Oliver, Audrey, a most vile
Mar-text. But Audrey, there is a youth here in the
Forest lays claim to you.

AUDREY: Ay, I know who 'tis: he hath no interest in me     30
in the world: here comes the man you mean.

*Enter William.*

CLOWN: It is meat and drink to me to see a clown, by my
troth, we that have good wits, have much to answer
for: we shall be flouting: we cannot hold.

5 WILLIAM: Good evening Audrey.

AUDREY: God ye good even William.

WILLIAM: And good even to you sir.

CLOWN: Good even gentle friend. Cover thy head, cover
thy head: nay prithee be cover'd. How old are you friend?

10 WILLIAM: Five and twenty sir.

CLOWN: A ripe age: is thy name William?

WILLIAM: William, sir.

CLOWN: A fair name. Wast born i'. th' Forest here?

WILLIAM: Ay sir, I thank God.

15 CLOWN: Thank God: a good answer: art rich?

WILLIAM: Faith sir, so, so.

CLOWN: So, so, is good, very good, very excellent good:
and yet it is not, it is but so, so: art thou wise?

WILLIAM: Ay, sir, I have a pretty wit.

20 CLOWN: Why, thou sayest well. I do now remember a saying: The fool doth think he is wise, but the wise man knows
himself to be a fool.   The heathen philosopher, when he
had a desire to eat a grape, would open his lips when he
put it into his mouth, meaning thereby, that grapes were

25 made to eat, and lips to open. You do love this maid?

WILLIAM: I do sir.

CLOWN: Give me your hand: art thou learned?

WILLIAM: No sir.

CLOWN: Then learn this of me, to have, is to have. For

30 it is a figure in rhetoric, that drink, being pour'd out of
a cup into a glass, by filling the one, doth empty the
other. For all your writers do consent, that *ipse* is he:
now you are not *ipse*, for I am he.

WILLIAM: Which he sir?

CLOWN: He sir, that must marry this woman: therefore
you clown, abandon: which is in the vulgar, leave the
society: which in the boorish, is company, of this female:
which in the common, is woman: which together, is, aban-  5
don the society of this female, or clown thou perishest:
or to thy better understanding, diest: or (to wit) I kill thee,
make thee away, translate thy life into death, thy liberty
into bondage: I will deal in poison with thee, or in bastinado, or in steel: I will bandy with thee in faction, I  10
will o'er-run thee with policy; I will kill thee a hundred
and fifty ways, therefore tremble and depart.

AUDREY: Do good William.

WILLIAM: God rest you merry sir.

*Exit.*  15
*Enter Corin.*

CORIN: Our master and mistress seeks you: come away,
away.

CLOWN: Trip Audrey, trip Audrey, I attend, I attend.

*Exeunt.*  20


V. 2


*Enter Orlando and Oliver.*

ORLANDO: Is't possible, that on so little acquaintance you
should like her? that, but seeing, you should love her?
and loving woo? And wooing, she should grant? And  25
will you persever to enjoy her?

OLIVER: Neither call the giddiness of it in question; the
poverty of her, the small acquaintance, my sudden wooing, nor her sudden consenting: but say with me, I love
Aliena: say with her, that she loves me: consent with  30
both, that we may enjoy each other: it shall be to your

good: for my father's house, and all the revenue, that was old Sir Rowland's will I estate upon you, and here live and die a shepherd.

*Enter Rosalind.*

5 ORLANDO: You have my consent. Let your wedding be to-morrow: thither will I invite the Duke, and all's contented followers: go you, and prepare Aliena; for look you, here comes my Rosalind.

ROSALIND: God save you brother.

10 OLIVER: And you fair sister.

*Exit.*

ROSALIND: Oh my dear Orlando, how it grieves me to see thee wear thy heart in a scarf.

ORLANDO: It is my arm.

15 ROSALIND: I thought thy heart had been wounded with the claws of a lion.

ORLANDO: Wounded it is, but with the eyes of a lady.

ROSALIND: Did your brother tell you how I counterfeited to sound, when he show'd me your handkercher?

20 ORLANDO: Ay, and greater wonders than that.

ROSALIND: O, I know where you are: nay, 'tis true: there was never any thing so sudden, but the fight of two rams, and Cæsar's thrasonical brag of I came, saw, and overcome. For your brother, and my sister, no sooner met,

25 but they look'd: no sooner look'd, but they lov'd; no sooner lov'd, but they sigh'd: no sooner sigh'd but they asked one another the reason: no sooner knew the reason, but they sought the remedy: and in these degrees, have they made a pair of stairs to marriage, which they

30 will climb incontinent, or else be incontinent before marriage; they are in the very wrath of love, and they will together. Clubs cannot part them.

ORLANDO: They shall be married to-morrow: and I will

bid the Duke to the nuptial. But O, how bitter a thing it
is, to look into happiness through another man's eyes:
by so much the more shall I to-morrow be at the height
of heart-heaviness, by how much I shall think my
brother happy, in having what he wishes for.                    5

ROSALIND: Why then to-morrow, I cannot serve your
turn for Rosalind?

ORLANDO: I can live no longer by thinking.

ROSALIND: I will weary you then no longer with idle talk·
ing. Know of me then (for now I speak to some purpose)   10
that I know you are a gentleman of good conceit: I speak
not this, that you should bear a good opinion of my
knowledge: insomuch (I say) I know you are: neither
do I labour for a greater esteem than may in some little
measure draw a belief from you, to do yourself good, and  15
not to grace me. Believe then, if you please, that I can
do strange things: I have since I was three year old con-
vers'd with a magician, most profound in his art, and yet
not damnable. If you do love Rosalind so near the heart,
as your gesture cries it out: when your brother marries  20
Aliena, shall you marry her. I know into what straits of
Fortune she is driven, and it is not impossible to me, if it
appear not inconvenient to you, to set her before your eyes
to-morrow, human as she is, and without any danger.

ORLANDO: Speak'st thou in sober meanings?                    25

ROSALIND: By my life I do, which I tender dearly, though
I say I am a magician: therefore put you in your best
array, bid your friends: for if you will be married to-
morrow, you shall: and to Rosalind if you will.

*Enter Silvius and Phebe.*                    30

Look, here comes a lover of mine, and a lover of hers.

PHEBE: Youth, you have done me much ungentleness,
To show the letter that I writ to you.

ROSALIND: I care not if I have: it is my study
    To seem despiteful and ungentle to you:
    You are there followed by a faithful shepherd,
    Look upon him, love him: he worships you.

5 PHEBE: Good shepherd, tell this youth what 'tis to love.

SILVIUS: It is to be all made of sighs and tears,
    And so am I for Phebe.

PHEBE: And I for Ganymede.

ORLANDO: And I for Rosalind.

10 ROSALIND: And I for no woman.

SILVIUS: It is to be all made of faith and service,
    And so am I for Phebe.

PHEBE: And I for Ganymede.

ORLANDO: And I for Rosalind.

15 ROSALIND: And I for no woman.

SILVIUS: It is to be all made of fantasy,
    All made of passion, and all made of wishes,
    All adoration, duty, and observance,
    All humbleness, all patience, and impatience,
20     All purity, all trial, all observance:
    And so am I for Phebe.

PHEBE: And so am I for Ganymede.

ORLANDO: And so am I for Rosalind.

ROSALIND: And so am I for no woman.

25 PHEBE: If this be so, why blame you me to love you?

SILVIUS: If this be so, why blame you me to love you?

ORLANDO: If this be so, why blame you me to love you?

ROSALIND: Why do you speak too, Why blame you me
    to love you?

30 ORLANDO: To her, that is not here, nor doth not hear.

ROSALIND: Pray you no more of this, 'tis like the howling
    of Irish wolves against the moon: I will help you if I
    can: I would love you if I could: to-morrow meet me

all together: I will marry you, if ever I marry woman,
and I'll be married to-morrow: I will satisfy you, if ever
I satisfi'd man, and you shall be married to-morrow. I
will content you, if what pleases you contents you, and
you shall be married to-morrow: as you love Rosalind  5
meet, as you love Phebe meet, and as I love no woman,
I'll meet; so fare you well: I have left you commands.

SILVIUS: I'll not fail, if I live.

PHEBE: Nor I.

ORLANDO: Nor I.  10

*Exeunt.*

# V. 3

*Enter Clown and Audrey.*

CLOWN: To-morrow is the joyful day Audrey, to-morrow
will we be married.  15

AUDREY: I do desire it with all my heart: and I hope it is
no dishonest desire, to desire to be a woman of the world?
Here come two of the banish'd Duke's pages.

*Enter two Pages.*

1 PAGE: Well met honest gentleman.  20

CLOWN: By my troth well met: come, sit, sit, and a song.

2 PAGE: We are for you, sit i' th' middle.

1 PAGE: Shall we clap into 't roundly, without hawking,
or spitting, or saying we are hoarse, which are the only
prologues to a bad voice.  25

2 PAGE: I' faith, i' faith, and both in a tune like two gipsies
on a horse.

SONG.

*It was a lover, and his lass,*
    *With a hey, and a ho, and a hey nonino,*  30
*That o'er the green corn-field did pass,*

In the spring time, the only pretty ring time,
When birds do sing, hey ding a ding, ding:
Sweet lovers love the spring.

Between the acres of the rye,
  5      With a hey, and a ho, and a hey nonino:
These pretty country folks would lie,
    In spring time, &c.

This carol they began that hour,
    With a hey and a ho, and a hey nonino:
10      How that a life was but a flower,
    In spring time, &c.

And therefore take the present time,
    With a hey, and a ho, and a hey nonino,
For love is crowned with the prime,
15      In spring time, &c.

CLOWN: Truly young gentlemen, though there was no great
matter in the ditty, yet the note was very untuneable.

I PAGE: You are deceiv'd sir, we kept time, we lost not
our time.

20  CLOWN: By my troth yes: I count it but time lost to hear
such a foolish song. God buy you, and God mend your
voices. Come Audrey.

*Exeunt.*

# V.4

25  *Enter Duke Senior, Amiens, Jaques, Orlando. Oliver,*
*Celia.*

DUKE SENIOR: Dost thou believe Orlando, that the boy
Can do all this that he hath promised?

ORLANDO: I sometimes do believe, and sometimes do not,
As those that fear they hope, and know they fear.
*Enter Rosalind, Silvius and Phebe.*
ROSALIND: Patience once more, whiles our compact is
urg'd:                                                                              5
You say, if I bring in your Rosalind,
You will bestow her on Orlando here?
DUKE SENIOR: That would I, had I kingdoms to give with
her.
ROSALIND: And you say you will have her, when I bring  10
her.
ORLANDO: That would I, were I of all kingdoms King.
ROSALIND: You say, you'll marry me, if I be willing.
PHEBE: That will I, should I die the hour after.
ROSALIND: But if you do refuse to marry me,                          15
You'll give yourself to this most faithful shepherd.
PHEBE: So is the bargain.
ROSALIND: You say that you'll have Phebe if she will.
SILVIUS: Though to have her and death, were both one
thing,                                                                              20
ROSALIND: I have promis'd to make all this matter even:
Keep you your word, O Duke, to give your daughter,
You yours Orlando, to receive his daughter:
Keep you your word Phebe, that you'll marry me,
Or else refusing me to wed this shepherd:                              25
Keep your word Silvius, that you'll marry her
If she refuse me, and from hence I go
To make these doubts all even.
*Exeunt Rosalind and Celia.*
DUKE SENIOR: I do remember in this shepherd boy,       30
Some lively touches of my daughter's favour.
ORLANDO: My lord, the first time that I ever saw him,
Methought he was a brother to your daughter:

But my good Lord, this boy is forest-born,
And hath been tutor'd in the rudiments
Of many desperate studies, by his uncle,
Whom he reports to be a great magician,

5                    *Enter Clown and Audrey.*

Obscured in the circle of this Forest.

JAQUES: There is sure another flood toward, and these
couples are coming to the Ark. Here comes a pair of
very strange beasts, which in all tongues, are call'd fools.

10 CLOWN: Salutation and greeting to you all.

JAQUES: Good my Lord, bid him welcome: this is the
motley-minded gentleman, that I have so often met in
the Forest: he hath been a courtier he swears.

CLOWN: If any man doubt that, let him put me to my

15 purgation, I have trod a measure, I have flattered a lady,
I have been politic with my friend, smooth with mine
enemy, I have undone three tailors, I have had four
quarrels, and like to have fought one.

JAQUES: And how was that ta'en up?

20 CLOWN: 'Faith we met, and found the quarrel was upon
the seventh cause.

JAQUES: How seventh cause? Good my Lord, like this
fellow.

DUKE SENIOR: I like him very well.

25 CLOWN: God 'ild you sir, I desire you of the like: I press
in here sir, amongst the rest of the country copulatives
to swear, and to forswear, according as marriage binds
and blood breaks: a poor virgin sir, an ill-favour'd thing
sir, but mine own, a poor humour of mine sir, to take that

30 that no man else will: rich honesty dwells like a miser
sir, in a poor house, as your pearl in your foul oyster.

DUKE SENIOR: By my faith, he is very swift, and sententious.

CLOWN: According to the fool's bolt sir, and such dulcet
diseases.

JAQUES: But for the seventh cause. How did you find the
quarrel on the seventh cause?

CLOWN: Upon a lie, seven times removed: (bear your    5
body more seeming Audrey) as thus sir: I did dislike the
cut of a certain courtier's beard: he sent me word, if I
said his beard was not cut well, he was in the mind it was:
this is call'd the retort courteous. If I sent him word
again, it was not well cut, he would send me word he    10
cut it to please himself: this is called the quip modest. If
again, it was not well cut, he disabled my judgement:
this is called, the reply churlish. If again it was not well
cut, he would answer I spake not true: this is call'd the
reproof valiant. If again, it was not well cut, he would    15
say, I lie: this is call'd the counter-check quarrelsome:
and so to the lie circumstantial, and the lie direct.

JAQUES: And how oft did you say his beard was not well
cut?

CLOWN: I durst go no further than the lie circumstantial:    20
nor he durst not give me the lie direct: and so we
measur'd swords, and parted.

JAQUES: Can you nominate in order now, the degrees of
the lie?

CLOWN: O sir, we quarrel in print, by the book: as you    25
have books for good manners: I will name you the
degrees. The first, the Retort courteous: the second, the
Quip modest; the third, the Reply churlish: the fourth,
the Reproof valiant: the fifth, the Countercheck quarrelsome: the sixth, the Lie with circumstance: the seventh,    30
the Lie direct: all these you may avoid, but the Lie direct:
and you may avoid that too, with an If. I knew when
seven Justices could not take up a quarrel, but when the

parties were met themselves, one of them thought but
of an If; as If you said so, then I said so: and they shook
hands, and swore brothers. Your If, is the only peace-
maker: much virtue in If.

5 JAQUES: Is not this a rare fellow my Lord? He's as good
at any thing, and yet a fool.

DUKE SENIOR: He uses his folly like a stalking-horse, and
under the presentation of that he shoots his wit.

*Enter Hymen, Rosalind, and Celia.*

10                        *Still Music.*

HYMEN: *Then is there mirth in heaven,*
*When earthly things made even*
*Atone together.*
*Good Duke receive thy daughter,*
15 *Hymen from Heaven brought her,*
*Yea brought her hither,*
*That thou mightst join her hand with his,*
*Whose heart within his bosom is.*

ROSALIND: To you I give myself, for I am yours.
20 To you I give myself, for I am yours.

DUKE SENIOR: If there be truth in sight, you are my
daughter.

ORLANDO: If there be truth in sight, you are my Rosalind.

PHEBE: If sight and shape be true, why then my love
25 adieu.

ROSALIND: I'll have no father, if you be not he:
I'll have no husband, if you be not he:
Nor ne'er wed woman, if you be not she.

HYMEN: Peace hoa: I bar confusion,
30 'Tis I must make conclusion
Of these most strange events:
Here's eight that must take hands,
To join in Hymen's bands,

If truth holds true contents.
You and you, no cross shall part;
You and you, are heart in heart:
You, to his love must accord,
Or have a woman to your Lord.                                    5
You and you, are sure together,
As the winter to foul weather:
Whiles a wedlock-hymn we sing,
Feed yourselves with questioning:
That reason, wonder may diminish                                 10
How thus we met, and these things finish.

### SONG.

*Wedding is great Juno's crown,*
 *O blessed bond of board and bed:*
*'Tis Hymen peoples every town,*                                 15
 *High wedlock then be honoured:*
*Honour, high honour and renown*
 *To Hymen, god of every town.*

DUKE SENIOR: O my dear niece, welcome thou art to me,
 Even daughter welcome, in no less degree.                       20
PHEBE: I will not eat my word, now thou art mine,
 Thy faith, my fancy to thee doth combine.
*Enter Second Brother.*
2 BROTHER: Let me have audience for a word or two:
 I am the second son of old Sir Rowland,                         25
 That bring these tidings to this fair assembly.
 Duke Frederick hearing how that every day
 Men of great worth resorted to this forest,
 Address'd a mighty power, which were on foot
 In his own conduct, purposely to take                           30
 His brother here, and put him to the sword:
 And to the skirts of this wild wood he came:
 Where, meeting with an old religious man,

After some question with him, was converted
Both from his enterprise, and from the world:
His crown bequeathing to his banish'd brother,
And all their lands restor'd to them again
5    That were with him exil'd. This to be true,
I do engage my life.

DUKE SENIOR: Welcome young man:
Thou offer'st fairly to thy brothers' wedding:
To one his lands withheld, and to the other
10   A land itself at large, a potent Dukedom.
First, in this Forest, let us do those ends
That here were well begun, and well begot:
And after, every of this happy number
That have endur'd shrewd days, and nights with us,
15   Shall share the good of our returned fortune,
According to the measure of their states,
Meantime, forget this new-fallen dignity,
And fall into our rustic revelry:
Play music, and you brides and bridegrooms all,
20   With measure heap'd in joy, to th' measures fall.

JAQUES: Sir, by your patience: if I heard you rightly,
The Duke hath put on a religious life,
And thrown into neglect the pompous Court.

2 BROTHER: He hath.

25 JAQUES: To him will I: out of these convertites,
There is much matter to be heard, and learn'd:
You to your former honour I bequeath:
Your patience, and your virtue, well deserves it.
You to a love, that your true faith doth merit:
30   You to your land, and love, and great allies:
You to a long, and well-deserved bed:
And you to wrangling, for thy loving voyage
Is but for two months victuall'd: so to your pleasures,

I am for other, than for dancing measures.

DUKE SENIOR: Stay, Jaques, stay.

JAQUES: To see no pastime, I: what you would have,
I'll stay to know, at your abandon'd cave.

*Exit.*                      5

DUKE SENIOR: Proceed, proceed: we'll begin these rites,
As we do trust, they'll end in true delights.

*Exeunt all but Rosalind.*

ROSALIND: It is not the fashion to see the Lady the Epilogue: but it is no more unhandsome, than to see the Lord   10
the Prologue. If it be true, that good wine needs no
bush, 'tis true, that a good play needs no Epilogue. Yet
to good wine they do use good bushes: and good plays
prove the better by the help of good Epilogues: what a
case am I in then, that am neither a good Epilogue, nor   15
cannot insinuate with you in the behalf of a good play?
I am not furnish'd like a beggar, therefore to beg will
not become me. My way is to conjure you, and I'll
begin with the women. I charge you (O women) for
the love you bear to men, to like as much of this play,   20
as please you: and I charge you (O men) for the love you
bear to women (as I perceive by your simpering, none
of you hates them) that between you, and the women,
the play may please. If I were a woman, I would kiss as
many of you as had beards that pleas'd me, complexions   25
that lik'd me, and breaths that I defi'd not: and I am
sure, as many as have good beards, or good faces, or
sweet breaths, will for my kind offer, when I make
curtsy, bid me farewell.

*Exit.*                      30

# NOTES

References are to the page and line of this edition: a full page contains 33 lines.

P. 23 L. 5    *on his blessing:* if he wished to receive his blessing.

P. 23 L. 7    *at school:* at the University.

P. 23 L. 16   *as much bound to him:* owe him as much gratitude, i.e. nothing.

P. 23 L. 20   *mines my gentility with my education:* undermines my breeding with lack of education.

P. 24 L. 6    *be naught:* be nothing, 'make yourself scarce'.

P. 24 L. 9    *prodigal portion ... penury:* 'have I spent my portion like the Prodigal Son who was obliged to feed swine and eat the husks with them?'

P. 24 L. 16   *courtesy of nations:* custom of civilized society.

P. 24 L. 21   *nearer to his reverence:* i.e. and so claiming greater respect.

P. 24 L. 23   *too young in this:* Here Oliver strikes Orlando, who loses his temper.

P. 25 L. 12   *your will:* your legacy and your wish.

P. 25 L. 22   *physic your rankness:* cure your excess of blood. 'Rankness' was a medical term for a condition requiring blood letting.

P. 27 L. 15   *grace himself on thee:* distinguish himself at your expense.

P. 27 L. 26   *go alone again:* i.e. he will be so crippled that he will always need support.

P. 29 L. 16   *Fortune reigns ... of Nature:* i.e. what comes to us – such as wealth or success – comes by Fortune, but beauty and honesty are natural gifts.

P. 29 L. 24   *Nature's natural:* a fool by nature.

P. 30 L. 28   *since the little wit that fools have ... great show:* on 4th June 1599 a number of books of satires were burnt in the Hall of the Stationers' Company. At the same

time it was ordered that no further satires or epi-
grams should be printed, nor English Histories, unless allowed by the Privy Council. The Council were
alarmed at the increasing number of satires and books
of history indirectly commenting on present troubles.

*Sport: of what colour:* Le Beau in his affected way
would pronounce 'sport' and 'spot' alike as 'spart'. — P. 31 L. 7

*rank:* place, but Rosalind puns on the other meaning
of 'strong scent', as of a fox. — P. 31 L. 13

*With bills ... these presents:* Rosalind makes a far- — P. 31 L. 27
fetched pun. Le Beau's 'presence' reminds her of
the common formula at the beginning of many legal
documents – *noverint universi per praesentes* – know
all men by these presents.

*broken music:* 'part music, concerted music; espec- — P. 32 L. 11
ially music to be performed by instruments of differ-
ent classes.' [*Shakespeare's England*, ii, 33] Rosalind
inevitably finds a pun in the phrase.

*out of suits:* not in the service of, i.e. out of favour. — P. 35 L. 20

*My better ... thrown down:* i.e. I am behaving as if I — P. 35 L. 24
had no manners.

*urg'd conference:* invited me to talk. — P. 36 L. 3

*humorous:* moody, see note on p. 83, l. 7. — P. 36 L. 12

*taller:* so the Folio reads, but later (p. 92, l. 20) Oliver — P. 36 L. 18
speaks of Celia as the shorter.

*in a better world than this:* 'when we live in safer — P. 36 L. 30
times.'

*lame me with reasons:* make me lame by throwing — P. 37 L. 11
arguments at me.

*kind of chase:* 'following such an argument.' — P. 38 L. 5

*take your change upon you:* bear your changed for- — P. 40 L. 17
tunes along.

*umber smirch my face:* Elizabethan ladies regarded an — P. 40 L. 27
ivory complexion as beautiful and so took elaborate
precautions to avoid sun tan. Amongst the country
folk the pale faces of Celia and Rosalind would have
been conspicuous.

P. 40 L. 32  *all points:* in every detail.

P. 41 L. 28  *old custom:* long experience.

P. 41 L. 31  *feel we not the penalty of Adam:* Many editors emend 'not' to 'but'. Professor Dover Wilson vindicates the reading; for if the Duke's remark be taken as a question, then its sense is 'Here we have the advantage of living natural lives, and the penalty of Adam – to feel the cold – is a good lesson to us'.

P. 42 L. 8  *toad ... precious jewel:* This was generally believed, and a 'toadstone' was regarded as an antidote to poison.

P. 42 L. 10  *exempt from public haunt:* free from crowds.

P. 42 L. 14  *translate ... sweet style:* take so tranquil a view of your harsh fortune.

P. 42 L. 19  *forked heads:* arrow heads.

P. 42 L. 22  *melancholy Jaques:* 'The origin of the name Jaques is fairly clear. It comes by an underground, not to say cloacal, channel from Sir John Harington's *Metamorphosis of Ajax* (1596). Harington was writing a scientific treatise on domestic sanitation in a Rabelaisian strain, and he used the name Ajax for the household offices. Thus, as he explains, AJAX = A JAX = A JAKES. But there is another connexion between Ajax and a jakes; both are melancholy, like the "melancholy of Moorditch" and such unsavoury similes.' The connexion between Jaques, Ajax and jakes (which is spelt 'jaques' in the 1st Quarto of *Lear*) can be brought closer in one of Harington's anecdotes. 'There was a very tall and serviceable Gentleman, sometime Lieutenant of the ordinance, called M. *Iaques Wingfield;* who comming one day, either of businesse, or of kindnes, to visit a great Lady of the Court, the Lady bad her gentlewoman ask, which of the *Wingfields* it was, *hee* tolde her *Iaques Wingfield:* the modest gentlewoman, that was not so well seene in the French, to knowe that *Iaques* was but *Iames* in English. who so bashfoole, that to mend the matter (as she thought) she brought her Lady worde, not without blushing, that it was M. *Privie Wingfield*, of which, I suppose the Lady then, I am sure the Gentleman after, as long as hee lived, was wont to make great sport.' [John Marston, *Scourge of Villainy*, 1599, ed. G. B. Harrison, p. 125.] Jaques is Shakespeare's contribution to the 'humour characters' so popular on the stage after Ben Jonson's *Every Man in his Humour* (1598); he is the melancholy critic of human follies.

| | |
|---|---|
| *consent and sufferance:* i.e. willing accomplices. | P. 44 L. 8 |
| *sanctified and holy traitors:* traitors who appear pious and holy. | P. 45 L. 15 |
| *diverted blood:* natural relationship gone wrong. | P. 46 L. 11 |
| *thrifty hire:* saved up pay. | P. 46 L. 13 |
| *unbashful forehead:* vicious boldness. | P. 46 L. 24 |
| *too late a week:* a week too late. | P. 47 L. 15 |
| *doublet and hose:* i.e. man's attire, for Rosalind is now dressed as 'Ganymede'. | P. 47 L. 26 |
| *no cross:* Elizabethan silver coins had a cross on the reverse side. Hence the common pun ' I bear no cross' = 'I have no money'. | P. 47 L. 30 |
| *bounds of feed:* pastures. | P. 50 L. 6 |
| *the beggarly thanks:* effusive gratitude like a beggar's. | P. 51 L. 21 |
| *despite of my invention:* in spite of my (small) power of imagination. | P. 52 L. 6 |
| *Ducdame:* this word is a trisyllable. Many ingenious attempts have been made to explain it, the latest being that it is a gipsy word meaning 'I tell fortunes'! More likely it is just one of those meaningless syllables, like 'hey nonny no', which fill out the line of many Elizabethan lyrics. Jaques' own explanation is that "'tis a Greek invocation to call fools into a circle' (i.e. to set fools gossiping), which it has, very successfully. | P. 52 L. 12 |
| *banquet:* in the Elizabethan sense of 'light refreshments'. | P. 52 L. 19 |

P. 53 L. 18    *compact of jars:* concorded of discords.

P. 53 L. 19    *discord in the spheres:* according to Pythagoras, whose
               astronomical notions were still generally accepted,
               the seven planets in their motion each emitted a
               different musical note, all together producing a
               heavenly harmony.

P. 53 L. 28    *a motley fool:* i.e. a professional fool wearing his
               parti-coloured costume.

P. 54 L. 1     *in good set terms:* in phrases carefully composed.

P. 54 L. 23    *remainder biscuit:* the hard dry biscuit left in store
               at the end of a voyage.

P. 54 L. 25    *vents In mangled forms:* utters with quaint turns of
               phrase.

P. 54 L. 33    *as large a charter:* as free a privilege. A charter was
               a special grant of privileges given by the king to a
               community or corporation.

P. 55 L. 7     *Not to seem:* the Folio omits 'not to', but both sense
               and metre need them.

P. 55 L. 19    *brutish sting:* i.e. lust.

P. 55 L. 20    *embossed sores, and headed evils:* boils and carbuncles
               caused by evil living.

P. 55 L. 24    *can therein tax any private party:* The satirists of the
               time when reproached for lampooning individuals
               often pleaded that they were attacking sin, not in-
               dividual sinners. Thus Marston in *The Scourge of
               Villainy* (1598) 'Gentle or ungentle hand that holdest
               mee, let not thine eye be cast upon privatnes, for I
               protest I glance not on it. Let this protestation satisfy
               our curious searchers. So may I obtaine my best
               hopes, as I am free from endevouring to blast any
               private man's good name. If any one (forced with
               his own guilt) will turn it home and say *Tis I*, I
               cannot hinder him. Neither do I injure him.' See note
               on Jaques (p. 42, l. 22).

P. 55 L. 26    *weary very means:* the phrase has not been satis-
               factorily emended or explained.

P. 55 L. 32    *basest function:* lowest kind of employment.

*his bravery ... cost:* his fine clothes have not cost me anything.   P. 55 L. 33

*You touched ... at first:* 'Your first guess is right; I am starving.'   P. 56 L. 17

*inland bred:* who knows civilization.   P. 56 L. 19

*All the world's a stage:* This is Shakespeare's little essay on the motto of the new Globe Theatre which the company had just occupied: *Totus mundus agit histrionem.*   P. 58 L. 1

*good capon lin'd:* i.e. bribed with the present of a fat chicken. It was a common complaint that those who wished for justice from country magistrates had to bring presents with them. Such magistrates were known as 'basket justices'.   P. 58 L. 16

*pantaloon:* the dotard of Italian comedy.   P. 58 L. 20

*absent argument ... thou present:* i.e. 'I would take my revenge on you.'   P. 60 L. 5

*quit thee:* release yourself from your obligation.   P. 60 L. 13

*thrice-crowned Queen of Night:* the divinity of the goddess Diana was threefold; for she was Luna the Moon in the sky, Diana the Huntress on earth, and Hecate in the underworld.   P. 60 L. 25

*private:* retired. The true Elizabethan courtier (and Touchstone 'hath been a courtier') lived gregarious and loathed solitude.   P. 61 L. 12

*good manners:* a quibble on the double meaning of 'polite behaviour' and 'good morals'.   P. 62 L. 3

*civet:* a perfume made from glandular secretions of the civet cat.   P. 62 L. 24

*make incision:* cut for bleeding.   P. 62 L. 31

*right butter-women's rank to market:* 'like a lot of old women ambling along to market.'   P. 63 L. 24

*false gallop:* canter – an apt simile for lame verses, as the motion of a canter goes 'titock, titock, titock'.   P. 64 L. 7

*medlar:* medlars, which are an acquired taste, are not eaten until they go soft.   P. 64 L. 12

*stretching of a span:* an echo of Psalm **xxxix** : 'Thou   P. 64 L. 26

hast made my days as it were a span long.' The span is the measurement of the outstretched hand from thumb to little finger.

P. 65 L. 1    *quintessence*: 'fifth essence', that which remains when the four elements have been taken away.

P. 65 L. 7    *Helen's cheek* ... : i.e. Rosalind is made up of the perfections of all the beauties of legend without their drawbacks.

P. 65 L. 9    *Atalanta*: a Greek maiden noted for her skill in running and her chastity; and so the pattern of chaste gracefulness.

P. 65 L. 17   *Jupiter*: some editors unnecessarily emend to 'pulpiter' = parson, but Rosalind is fond of swearing by Jupiter. (See p. 47, l. 22 and p. 49, l. 13.)

P. 65 L. 23   *scrip and scrippage*: the scrip is a shepherd's pouch. Touchstone accordingly invents a phrase based on 'bag and baggage'.

P. 66 L. 5    *Pythagoras' time ... Irish rat*: referring to the notion of Pythagoras that souls could transmigrate into the bodies of animals. It was a popular belief that Irish witches could rhyme man and beast to death.

P. 66 L. 20   *out of all hooping*: beyond even a cry of astonishment.

P. 66 L. 24   *South-sea of discovery*: i.e. 'as endless as the South Sea to one on a voyage of discovery'.

P. 67 L. 18   *Gargantua*: the giant of Rabelais' enormous work.

P. 68 L. 6    *sing ... without a burthen*: i.e. 'don't keep interrupting'. *Burthen*: the refrain of a song.

P. 68 L. 7    *bring'st me out*: put'st me out.

P. 68 L. 17   *God buy you*: This is the usual Folio spelling of the phrase; sometimes altered to 'God be wi' you'.

P. 68 L. 22   *ill-favouredly*: with a wry face.

P. 68 L. 31   *conned them out of rings*: It was a pretty custom to inscribe little messages (or posies) in rings.

P. 68 L. 33   *right painted cloth*: In taverns and rooms for which tapestry would be too costly, cloths painted with scriptural or classical scenes were used to cover the walls. The figures were sometimes provided with texts or labels issuing from their mouths containing suitable phrases.

*inland*: living near a city, and so cultured.     P. 70 L. 33

*cage of rushes*: a cage made of reeds for small birds.     P. 71 L. 22

*A lean cheek ... desolation*: These are all the marks of     P. 71 L. 25 the melancholic and hopeless lover. Thus Valentine In *Two Gentlemen of Verona* is rebuked by Speed: 'first, you have learned, like Sir Proteus, to wreathe your arms like a malecontent; to relish a love-song, like a robin-redbreast; to walk alone, like one that had the pestilence; to sigh, like a schoolboy that had lost his A B C; to weep, like a young wench that had buried her grandam; to fast, like one that takes diet; to watch, like one that fears robbing; to speak puling, like a beggar at Hallowmass. You were wont, when you laughed, to crow like a cock; when you walked, to walk like one of the lions; when you fasted, it was presently after dinner; when you looked sadly, it was for want of money; and now you are metamorphosed with a mistress, that, when I look on you, I can hardly think you my master.'

Hamlet, when rejected by Ophelia, behaves as Orlando should. (Act 2, Scene 1.)

*blue eye*: i.e. with dark lines round the eye.     P. 71 L. 25

*unquestionable*: glum, not to be spoken to.     P. 71 L. 26

*your having in beard ... revenue*: Your beard any-     P. 71 L. 29 how is not worth much.

*point-device in your accoutrements*: very neat in your     P. 71 L. 33 dress.

*dark house, and a whip*: the common treatment of     P. 72 L. 18 lunatics.

*liver as clean*: the liver was regarded as the seat of     P. 73 L. 4 passion.

*capricious*: goatlike (from Latin *caper*, a he-goat),     P. 73 L. 25 lascivious, with a pun on 'Goths'.

*a great reckoning in a little room*: i.e. a huge bill for a     P. 73 L. 30 private dinner-party. The little private room in a great house or inn is sometimes used as a poetic image, very effective when most men lived in public. Thus Barrabas, in Marlowe's play, *The Jew of Malta*, speaks of his precious jewels as 'infinite riches in a little room', and Donne in *The Goodmorrow*:

> 'For love all love of other sights controls
> And makes one little room an everywhere.'

P. 74 L. 12   *honesty ... sauce to sugar*: Touchstone's argument is that it is too sickly for a man of the world when a pretty girl is particular.

P. 74 L. 30   *horn-beasts*: The inevitable Elizabethan joke on cuckolds who were supposed to wear horns as a sign of their misfortune.

P. 75 L. 8   *horn ... to want*: with a pun on the *cornucopia*, or horn of plenty.

P. 76 L. 19   *dissembling colour ... Judas's*: Judas Iscariot was depicted with red hair which denoted lechery and disloyalty.

P. 77 L. 20   *quite traverse*: i.e. the glancing blow of one who is afraid to charge 'full tilt' at his opponent.

P. 79 L. 2   *capable impressure*: perceptible imprint.

P. 79 L. 20   *see no more ... dark to bed*: 'You're not so brilliant that you can go to bed by your own light.'

P. 79 L. 24   *ordinary Of Nature's sale-work*: 'very common goods.'

P. 79 L. 28   *black silk hair*: 'In the old age black was not counted fair' (Sonnet 127).

P. 79 L. 32   *foggy south*: south wind, believed to bring illness.

P. 80 L. 11   *Foul ... scoffer*: 'you are ugly anyway, and uglier when you are disdainful.'

P. 80 L. 31   *Who ever lov'd that lov'd not at first sight*: The line is a touching and deliberate reminder of Marlowe, being quoted from his *Hero and Leander* which was first published in 1598, five years after Marlowe's death. The lines run:

> Where both deliberate the love is slight:
> Whoever lov'd that lov'd not at first sight.

*omittance is no quittance:* 'because I let him off now,    P. 82 L. 18
it does not mean that he will get off altogether.'

*a melancholy fellow:* The word 'humour', like the    P. 82 L. 31
modern 'complex', had become popular in intellectual jargon. It was a misuse of a medical term. The
theory of medicine was based on the conception that
man's physical health was controlled by four 'humours', or principles, of which all matter was compounded – i.e. earth, air, fire, and water. In the body
the corresponding humours were black bile, blood,
bile, and phlegm. So long as the humours were
equally balanced the body was healthy, but if one
predominated, then both body and mind were affected, and the patient suffered from a melancholy,
sanguine, choleric or phlegmatic humour. The word
was, however, used to denote any oddity of behaviour, and the fop would justify the use of a fantastic
ruff or hatband as 'his humour'.

  'Ask Humours why a feather he doth wear?
   It is his humour, by the Lord, he'll swear.'

But of all affectations of humour, the melancholic
humour was most in fashion, and showed that the
sufferer was an intellectual. The outward signs of
the complaint were a large black hat, a cloak, and a
moody aloofness. Thus in *Every Man in his Humour*
Matheo is impressed when he hears that Stephano is
melancholy and observes, 'O Lord, sir, it's your only
best humour, sir; your true melancholy breeds your
perfect wit, sir. I am melancholy myself divers times,
sir, and then do I no more but take your pen and
paper presently, and write you your half score or
your dozen of sonnets at a sitting.'

  To which Stephano replies, 'I thank you, sir; I
shall be bold I warrant you; have you a close stool
there?' – for this piece of furniture was peculiarly
devoted to melancholy contemplations. Similarly
John Davies in his epigram *On a Gull* begins:

> See yonder melancholy gentleman,
> Which hoodwink'd with his hat alone doth sit,
> Think what he thinks, and tell me if you can,
> What great affairs trouble his little wit.

Even in Milton's youth, melancholy was the proper pose for *Il Penseroso*, the grave student. The contemporary text-book on the subject is Burton's *Anatomy of Melancholy*, 1621.

P. 83 L. 3    *modern censure*: trifling criticism.

P. 83 L. 7    *scholar's melancholy ... emulation*: i.e. jealous rivalry. This is still true, as can be seen from the book reviews in any learned journal.

P. 83 L. 28   *Farewell Monsieur Traveller*: ... *lisp*: ... These were the common gibes against the returned traveller.

P. 83 L. 28   *lisp*: talk with a foreign accent.

P. 83 L. 32   *swam in a gondola*: been to Venice.

P. 84 L. 8    *clapp'd ... shoulder*: i.e. made an arrest.

P. 84 L. 20   *armed in his fortune ... wife*: i.e. the snail has horns before marriage and so forestalls the slanders which his wife will bring him.

P. 85 L. 17   *by attorney*: by proxy.

P. 85 L. 17   *the poor world ... Hero of Sestos*: No one, says Rosalind, has truly died for love. Even the great lovers of legend, such as Troilus who was madly in love with Cressida, or Leander who swam across the Hellespont to sleep with Hero, died from other causes, in spite of what the historians say.

P. 86 L. 23   *girl goes before the priest*: i.e. anticipates the priest's words in her eagerness.

P. 87 L. 22   *that woman ... husband's occasion*: that cannot blame her husband as the cause of her own faults.

P. 88 L. 21   *unknown bottom*: too deep to be sounded.

P. 88 L. 25   *bastard of Venus*: Cupid.

P. 89 L. 13   In printing this Song, I follow the arrangement suggested by Professor Dover Wilson. Other editors print 'the rest shall bear' as a stage direction. In the Folio 'Then sing ... burthen' is printed as one line.

*rare as phœnix*: According to the legend there was only one phœnix. It lived for five hundred years. Then it built itself a nest of spices which was set alight by the rapid beating of its wings; and from the ashes came forth a new phœnix.    P. 90 L. 13

*leathern hand*: i.e. the hand of a working woman, not a lady.    P. 90 L. 21

*seal up thy mind*: write your answer and send it by him.    P. 91 L. 23

*female favour*: girlish face.    P. 92 L. 19

*indented glides*: wavy motion.    P. 93 L. 13

*udders all drawn dry*: i.e. hungry and fierce.    P. 93 L. 15

*Clubs cannot part them*: when a brawl occurred in London streets, there was a cry of 'clubs'. Thereupon the apprentices seized their clubs and swarmed out to separate the parties.    P. 98 L. 32

*not damnable*: i.e. his magic was beneficent not malicious.    P. 99 L. 19

*straits of Fortune*: difficult position.    P. 99 L. 21

*done me much ungentleness*: You have not behaved like a gentleman towards me.    P. 99 L. 32

*clap into 't*: start at once.    P. 101 L. 23

*only prologues*: usual apologies.    P. 101 L. 24

*Song*: The Folio prints the last stanza (And therefore, etc.) after the 6th line of the Song, but other existing versions show the correct order.    P. 101 L. 28

*ring time*: wedding-bell time.    P. 102 L. 1

*compact is urg'd*: agreement is repeated.    P. 103 L. 4

*purgation*: clearing from an accusation.    P. 104 L. 15

*trod a measure*: i.e. taken my part in a dance. Dancing was an essential accomplishment of a courtier.    P. 104 L. 15

*undone three tailors*: i.e. by not paying their bills.    P. 104 L. 17

*disabled my judgement*: said my judgement was weak.    P. 105 L. 12

*lie direct*: the lie direct – 'you are a liar' – was the quickest way to provoke a duel. Any man who refused to fight on receiving it branded himself    P. 105 L. 17

coward. This kind of argument was quite seriously propounded in books on duelling.

**P. 106 L. 7** *stalking-horse:* a real or imitation horse used as cover when stalking.

**P 106 L. 9** *Enter Hymen:* It has been suggested that this little masque of Hymen (the god of marriage) is quite out of place in the story and was added for some performance at Court. It can be cut without interfering with the action.

**P. 109 L. 11** *good wine ... bush:* An old proverb, arising from the custom of vintners of hanging up a bush as the sign of their trade.

**P. 109 L. 24** *If I were a woman:* Rosalind in Shakespeare's day was played by a boy. There were no professional actresses on the English stage before the Restoration.

# GLOSSARY

*acquit*: distinguish; *lit.* get a favourable verdict.

*allotery*: portion.

*along*: at full length.

*anatomize*: dissect.

*antique*: ancient, 'good old'

*assayed*: attempted.

*atomies*: motes in the sunbeam.

*atone*: make at one.

*bandy*: contend.

*bastinado*: thrashing – a fashionable word at the time.

*batler*: bat used for washing clothes.

*bear with*: be patient with.

*bestows*: behaves.

*blow on*: censure.

*bob*: rap on the knuckles.

*boisterous*: threatening.

*bonnet*: hat.

*breath'd*: exercised.

*breather*: living creature.

*bugle*: bead.

*calling*: name.

*caparisoned*: equipped.

*carelessly*: without a care.

*carlot*: churl.

*cast*: cast off.

*character*: (*vb.*) write; (*noun*) handwriting.

*chopt*: chapped.

*civil*: 1. sober, serious; 2. civilized.

*civility*: civilized behaviour.

*clown*: rustic.

*cod*: pod.

*comfortable*: of good comfort.

*coming on*: encouraging.

*commission*: authority.

*conceit*: imagination.

*confines*: territories.

*conjure*: win over by magic.

*conned*: learnt by heart.

*constant*: faithful.

*contract*: formal bethrothal.

*contriver*: plotter.

*cony*: rabbit.

*cope*: encounter.

*cote*: cottage.

*countenance*: favour.

*counterfeit*: pretend.

*cousin*: see COZ.

*cover*: lay the table.

*coz*: cousin, but used of any relation.

*cross*: trouble.

*curtle-axe*: cutlass.

*damask*: the pink of damask roses.

*dearly*: at great cost.

*defied*: disliked.

*derive*: acquire by descent.

*device*: thought.

*despite* : spite.

*dial* : watch.

*disable* : make slighting remarks about.

*disputable* : argumentative.

*dog-apes* : baboons.

*dole* : lamentation.

*emulator* : jealous rival.

*enforcement* : means of forcing.

*engage* : pledge.

*entertainment* : hospitality.

*exercises* : training.

*extent* : legal seizure.

*eyne* : eye.

*fall* : round, bout.

*fancy-monger* : trader in love.

*fantasy* : 1. love ; 2. imagination.

*fashion* : manner.

*fells* : fleeces.

*fleet* : spend.

*flux* : flow.

*foul* : plain.

*free* : guiltless.

*function* : occupation.

*furnished* : equipped.

*galled* : rubbed sore.

*gentle* : gentlemanly.

*God 'ild you* : God reward you.

*graff* : graft.

*gravell'd* : run aground.

*gross band* : vile company

*hard-favoured* : plain faced.

*hawking* : clearing the throat.

*hem* : cough up.

*hinds* : servants.

*homily* : sermon

*honest* : chaste.

*hurtling* : confusion, noise of combat.

*husbandry* : economy.

*hyen* : hyena.

*ill-favoured* : ugly.

*incontinent* : immediately.

*inquisition* : search.

*insinuate* : ingratiate oneself.

*instance* : give example.

*invectively* : with bitter satire.

*kindness* : natural affection.

*leer* : look .

*lief* : 'as lief', as soon.

*lieu* : stead.

*liked* : pleased.

*limn'd* : painted.

*love-shaked* : i.e. by the fever.

*manage* : training.

*material* : full of matter.

*matter* : good sense.

*measure* : dance.

*meed* : reward.

*misconsters* : misconstrues.

*misprised* : considered worthless.

*modern instances* : commonplace illustrations.

*moonish* : changeable as the moon.

*moralize:* make moral comments on.

*naught:* bad, worthless.
*new fangled:* eager for novelties
*nurture:* good breeding.

*observance:* devotion.

*pageant:* play.
*painted:* artificial.
*parcels:* parts.
*parlous:* perilous.
*passing:* exceedingly.
*peascod:* pea pod, pea plant.
*perpend:* consider.
*petitionary:* pleading.
*ply:* press, work on.
*poke:* pocket.
*policy:* underhand means.
*politic:* crafty.
*pompous:* ceremonious.
*power:* army.
*practice:* plot.
*presence:* appearance.
*presently:* immediately.
*priser:* prize fighter.
*proper:* handsome.
*puisny:* paltry, inexperienced.
*purgation:* oath of innocence; proof.
*purlieus:* boundaries.

*quail:* shrink.
*question:* conversation.
*quintain:* a block, resembling a human figure, used for tilting practice.

*quotidian:* fever recurring daily.

*ragged:* rough.
*railed on:* abused.
*range:* wander.
*rank:* row.
*rankness:* excessive growth.
*rascal:* young deer in poor condition.
*raw:* unripe, simple.
*reck:* care.
*recountments:* exchange of tales.
*remorse:* pity.
*removed:* remote.
*render:* give back.
*roynish:* rude.

*sad brow:* seriousness.
*saws:* sayings.
*sentence:* proverbial or wise saying.
*sententious:* file of 'sentences
*sequester'd:* separated.
*shrewd:* bitter.
*simples:* drugs, ingredients
*smother:* thin smoke.
*sound:* swoon.
*spare:* frugal.
*speed:* aid.
*squandering:* haphazard.
*stays:* keeps at home.
*still:* always.
*swashing:* swaggering.
*synod:* council.

*taxation*: satire.
*tempered*: compounded.
*tenour*: intention.
*toy*: trifle.
*trow*: know.

*unbanded*: without a band.
*uncouth*: savage.
*unexpressive*: inexpressible.

*uses*: advantages.

*velvet*: velvet-coated, sleek.
*vents*: utters.
*verge*: edge.

*warp*: freeze.
*whetstone*: sharpener.
*wind*: turn.

# PENGUIN POPULAR CLASSICS

*Published or forthcoming*

| | |
|---|---|
| **Joseph Conrad** | Heart of Darkness |
| | Lord Jim |
| | Nostromo |
| | The Secret Agent |
| | Victory |
| **James Fenimore Cooper** | The Last of the Mohicans |
| **Stephen Crane** | The Red Badge of Courage |
| **Daniel Defoe** | Moll Flanders |
| | Robinson Crusoe |
| **Charles Dickens** | Bleak House |
| | The Christmas Books |
| | David Copperfield |
| | Great Expectations |
| | Hard Times |
| | Little Dorrit |
| | Martin Chuzzlewit |
| | Nicholas Nickleby |
| | The Old Curiosity Shop |
| | Oliver Twist |
| | The Pickwick Papers |
| | A Tale of Two Cities |
| **Fyodor Dostoyevsky** | Crime and Punishment |
| **George Eliot** | Adam Bede |
| | Middlemarch |
| | The Mill on the Floss |
| | Silas Marner |
| **John Meade Falkner** | Moonfleet |
| **Henry Fielding** | Tom Jones |
| **F. Scott Fitzgerald** | The Diamond as Big as the Ritz |
| | The Great Gatsby |
| | Tender is the Night |
| **Gustave Flaubert** | Madame Bovary |
| **Elizabeth Gaskell** | Cousin Phillis |
| | Cranford |
| | Mary Barton |
| | North and South |
| **Kenneth Grahame** | The Wind in the Willows |